Stacey Demarco

2023
LUNAR
& SEASONAL DIARY

Northern Hemisphere

R ROCKPOOL
rockpoolpublishing.com

'*Everything is fruit to me that your seasons bring, Nature. All things come of you, have their being in you and return to you.*'

Marcus Aurelius, Stoic philosopher, *Meditations*: Book IV, 23

A Rockpool book
PO Box 252 Summer Hill
NSW 2130
Australia
rockpoolpublishing.com
Follow us! 🅵 🅸 rockpoolpublishing
Tag your images with #rockpoolpublishing

Published in 2022 by Rockpool Publishing
Copyright text © Stacey Demarco, 2022
Copyright design © Rockpool Publishing, 2022
Design by Sara Lindberg, Rockpool Publishing
Typeset by Daniel Poole, Rockpool Publishing
Cover design by Kinga Britschgi
Edited by Heather Millar
Author photo by Jason Corroto
Images from Shutterstock

ISBN 978-1-925946-65-9
Northern hemisphere edition

Printed and bound in China
10 9 8 7 6 5 4 3 2 1

JANUARY
M	T	W	T	F	S	S
						1
2	3	4	5	6	7	8
9	10	11	12	13	14	15
16	17	18	19	20	21	22
23	24	25	26	27	28	29
30	31					

FEBRUARY
M	T	W	T	F	S	S
		1	2	3	4	5
6	7	8	9	10	11	12
13	14	15	16	17	18	19
20	21	22	23	24	25	26
27	28					

MARCH
M	T	W	T	F	S	S
		1	2	3	4	5
6	7	8	9	10	11	12
13	14	15	16	17	18	19
20	21	22	23	24	25	26
27	28	29	30	31		

APRIL
M	T	W	T	F	S	S
					1	2
3	4	5	6	7	8	9
10	11	12	13	14	15	16
17	18	19	20	21	22	23
24	25	26	27	28	29	30

MAY
M	T	W	T	F	S	S
1	2	3	4	5	6	7
8	9	10	11	12	13	14
15	16	17	18	19	20	21
22	23	24	25	26	27	28
29	30	31				

JUNE
M	T	W	T	F	S	S
			1	2	3	4
5	6	7	8	9	10	11
12	13	14	15	16	17	18
19	20	21	22	23	24	25
26	27	28	29	30		

JULY
M	T	W	T	F	S	S
					1	2
3	4	5	6	7	8	9
10	11	12	13	14	15	16
17	18	19	20	21	22	23
24	25	26	27	28	29	30
31						

AUGUST
M	T	W	T	F	S	S
	1	2	3	4	5	6
7	8	9	10	11	12	13
14	15	16	17	18	19	20
21	22	23	24	25	26	27
28	29	30	31			

SEPTEMBER
M	T	W	T	F	S	S
				1	2	3
4	5	6	7	8	9	10
11	12	13	14	15	16	17
18	19	20	21	22	23	24
25	26	27	28	29	30	

OCTOBER
M	T	W	T	F	S	S
						1
2	3	4	5	6	7	8
9	10	11	12	13	14	15
16	17	18	19	20	21	22
23	24	25	26	27	28	29
30	31					

NOVEMBER
M	T	W	T	F	S	S
		1	2	3	4	5
6	7	8	9	10	11	12
13	14	15	16	17	18	19
20	21	22	23	24	25	26
27	28	29	30			

DECEMBER
M	T	W	T	F	S	S
			1	2	3	
4	5	6	7	8	9	10
11	12	13	14	15	16	17
18	19	20	21	22	23	24
25	26	27	28	29	30	31

ACKNOWLEDGEMENTS

At the beginning of each year, we usually move forward with some optimism and hope. It's often the feeling we get when we begin something new, where we get to seek, try, engage, flow forward once again into an untold story.

I like to think that all of us who are together again through this diary can weave our magic with some connection and optimism as we travel through the sacred pathways of the moon and seasons. This diary is for you who seek the harmony of this journey.

As always, my gratitude extends to my husband Adam and my agent Richard Martin for their ongoing support. A huge expression of wonder and thanks to Kinga Britschgi for her beautiful cover. A thank you to my publisher Lisa Hanrahan and her team at Rockpool Publishing.

And finally, I am often asked how to honour the gods or goddesses that we feel closest to. Often of course the answer is particular to that deity, however, I have learned that dedicating our everyday and practical actions or projects to them is one of the highest kinds of reciprocity. As always, then, this work is dedicated, as it has been since the first edition, to my patroness, the goddess Artemis.

HOW TO USE THIS DIARY

Welcome to a new year and a diary with a difference!

Remember when you were a small child and you were told all kinds of strange stories about things?

It is a distinct memory of mine sitting with my dad under a night sky and him showing me the face of the 'man in the moon' and telling me that there was indeed a man up there who looks down at us. I remember being fascinated but slightly concerned. I mean, poor moon fellow – he must be lonely and, wait, can he see me all the time?

Later, I also remember my grandmother pointing up at that same moon and showing me the rabbit in the moon, explaining where his face and ears were and why he was there. Later again, someone at school told me the moon was made of cheese. Then, over a long time, I have been told that the moon has aliens, that it is hollow and even that it's actually just a hologram. That last one is particularly weird, because without the balancing gravitational pull of the moon the earth would be in big trouble!

Now, while I absolutely adore the mythos of the rabbit in the moon, I rationally know there is no actual rabbit in the moon. I have unlearned as well as learned about the moon (and much else) as time goes by. It is important to learn and unlearn continually if we are to grow and gain true wisdom. Right now, lunar magic and how to work with the moon is very much in fashion. I've been creating this diary for 13 years (and counting), and when we began interest was not so strong. The internet has grown and we have social media platforms that allow anyone and everyone to have their opinion and propagate all kinds of information about the moon in magical workings.

I am so truly excited that more and more people are getting turned on to the advantages of working with lunar cycles, but it's more important than ever to have good-quality information to learn from and travel along with. The first thing that has always been an important intention for me with this diary is that it demonstrates that the moon doesn't work alone in magic, and that of course every moon is a magical moon. The alchemy of magic is such that the lunar energies get combined with local seasonal energies and other powerful earthly elements and, whoa, we get the real magical deal!

The second important intention is that I want you to see that you were a big part of the magic. I have never wanted to get overly complex with rows and rows of coordinates because I want you to create into this work yourself. YOU as magic. This means I give you quality guidelines and structures and you create into this. I don't tell you what to do; instead, you create into the structure. And, so, all the information inside here can be used in practical ways as the year progresses and changes from season to season, month to month.

This seasonal and lunar diary is designed to help you to connect deeply with your birthright of lunar and seasonal energies. It gives you all the timings and information that I believe is most relevant and effective for most modern people in progressing themselves and their magic. The clear marking of dark, new and full moon phases throughout the weeks and a daily update on whether the moon is waxing or waning is an easy way to keep on top of the most advantageous energetic timings for everything from spellcasting, growing and harvesting plants, cutting your hair, healing, inviting health and vitality for your body or creating personalised ritual.

There is also a god or goddess of the month to explore and learn from and a process for working with them for you to try. I know this is one of the most loved inclusions of the diary and I always try to offer you a mix of well-known and more obscure (yet powerful) deities to explore.

To keep your momentum going, at the beginning of each month there is a section to keep track of your ideas and intentions, so you can take true action to bring them from thought to reality with more ease.

While this diary gives you a lot of information to work with for even the most experienced practitioner, it is created for anyone who has an interest in how practical magic can transform their lives for the better.

So, I give you my continued commitment to provide you with reliable lunar, seasonal and pagan wisdom you can actually use in real life. This diary can then indeed be a magical companion throughout your year that you can rely on, be inspired by and that will support you in your intentions ongoing.

No matter what moon phase it is or what season, this diary helps you to make BIG magic.

With great love

Stacey Demarco

THE MODERN WITCH

ABOUT SPELLCRAFT

How and why do spells work? This is a big question that can be answered! For a detailed explanation check out the chapter that answers this in my book *There's a Witch in the Boardroom.* The short answer is dependent on whether you wish to go the spiritual or scientific route. Or both!

THE SPIRITUAL PATH

Witches and those from many other spiritual paths believe that we are connected to all things, including the Divine. The Divine assists us in achieving our intentions when we communicate effectively what it is that we want or don't want. To perform spellcraft we need to clearly state what our intentions are and raise considerable energy around this intention before releasing it in a directed fashion. We then take steps towards what we need and desire and the Divine meets us more than halfway. Magic happens. We get what we want.

THE SCIENTIFIC PATH

Spells speak the language of the subconscious. The subconscious is the part of the mind that directs us towards our goals and dreams. It's where ideas pop up from and where creativity is based. You can 'program' the subconscious to focus on what you want through elements such as symbology, movement, visualisation and emotion. Spells are a great way to do this effectively.

Whatever explanation you prefer, or a little bit of both, know that spells, rituals and invocations work effectively.

FIVE TOP CASTING TIPS

1. Relax, have fun! One of the best ways to ensure powerful spellcraft is to leave all your administration, worries and preconceived ideas behind and just let go! Spellcraft is meant to be a joyful practice. Even when we may be casting to rid ourselves of something we no longer need, there is at least a feeling of satisfaction or hope that things will now change for the better.

2. Don't worry if things don't go perfectly. So, what if the candle blows out or the incense doesn't light or your phone rings? Does that mean your spell is ruined? Well, only if you stop! Spells are more about knowing what you want and raising power behind this than whether or not things run perfectly. Be confident. Hold your intention clearly and keep going!

3. Plan in advance. Sometimes a quickly planned spell is a good spell, but when you can, plan ahead, especially when it comes to timings. This diary gives you great timing information that you can use to pinpoint the best days to cast for your particular needs. Ensuring that you have any ingredients or supplies ahead of time also reduces your stress levels and leaves you free to concentrate on your intentions.

I also think that it's important to plan for safety, for example, keeping children and animals away from flames, flames away from your animals and kids, using good-quality magical supplies, which you may have to order, and having the room well ventilated when using incense. Most important, though, is to plan by being crystal clear about what you are casting for! Your intention is of utmost importance. (By the way, if you don't know what you want, cast for clarity!) Take the time before starting to cast to examine what it is that you want (or don't want) and put this in clear, concise language. After all, if you don't know what you want, the universe can't co-create properly with you!

4. Don't interfere with free will. It is a terrible misconception that witchcraft is commonly used to directly control someone's mind or actions. One of the key tenets of most witchcraft traditions is to never interfere with another's free will. Spellcraft works very effectively, so it is not fair to impose our will, or what we believe is the best thing for someone else, upon another person. This means we don't cast on or for other people as it may have consequences. Even if someone is ill, I always ask permission before commencing any kind of healing invocation. If they are very ill and can't give permission I always add the direction '… if it be for the good of all', as a kind of insurance policy.

Love spells are probably the trickiest when it comes to ensuring free will is intact. No matter what, we never cast for a particular person; instead, we cast for the kind of relationship and partner we desire. This means we attract the best candidate – who may or may not be the person we know!

5. Participate! Equally important as having a clear intention is participating after the spell. This is a chance for you to get moving, choosing in the direction of your intention!

After a spell is almost complete, I always like to ask the Divine for suggestions on what to do next. The way this request is answered is rarely a big booming voice that tells you clearly what to do! Instead, it comes like ideas do … effortlessly and easily. It's a kind of 'popping into your head' feeling. By actioning any or all of these 'messages' we are co-creating with the Divine. This means you start moving. Even a small start has a ripple effect that will lead you to your intention more quickly.

SPELLCASTING MADE EASY

Everyone can cast! Here is a **spellcasting template** to assist you to write your own spell. Everyone can write an effective spell if they follow these outlines. Each spell has a 'skeleton' – a structure that gives the spell form and function. Fill in this template and you have the beginnings of a great spell! And, remember, be creative, confident and have fun!

1. Focus
(This is where you begin to decide to cast a spell for a specific reason and to plan the process, taking into consideration time and ethics. This can include a list of things you'll need to cast the spell.)

2. Purpose and intention
(Clearly and concisely state what the spell is for and what you hope to manifest e.g. Great goddess, I am here to ask you to help me achieve XYZ, quickly and easily. Or: Universe, I wish to attract my ideal partner for a committed relationship leading to marriage.)

3. Raising power
(This is how you'll raise energy to boost your intention. Common ways are raising emotion, meditation, drumming, dancing and moving.)

4. Release
(This is how you will release and send all that power you have raised out in to the universe. It should be different to how you have raised power e.g. burning something, clapping, shouting, stopping the movement suddenly.)

5. Participation and grounding
(This is the next step you'll take in the physical world to start manifesting what you want. Also, we often feel filled with energy after casting and sometimes we may wish to ground that energy a little. Great ways to do this include having a bath or shower, placing our hands on the ground or on a plant or eating.)

SPELL TIMINGS AND MOON CYCLES

One of the most common questions around spellcasting is that of timing: **'What is the best time to cast my spells?'**

The simple answer is *any time*. However, there are particular times that are seen as more powerful, and if we align ourselves with them they can assist us in achieving greater success. As we honour the earth and creation, we closely observe the cycles of nature as our guide. These include the moon cycles, seasonal changes and the position of the sun in the sky.

Traditionally, witches and pagans work closely with moon energy, which encompasses both the moon phases and the tides. This diary gives you clear information about moon phases and offers suggestions about what to cast for as well. You can check tidal information with your local newspaper, weather channel or specialist website (see the Resources section at the back of this diary).

MOON PHASE TIMINGS 2023

DARK MOON	NEW MOON	FULL MOON
—	—	6 January, 6.07 pm
20 January	21 January, 3.53 pm	5 February, 1.28 pm
19 February	20 February, 2.05 am	7 March, 7.40 am
20 March	21 March, 1.23 pm	6 April, 12.34 am
19 April	20 April, 12.12 am	5 May, 1.34 pm
18 May	19 May, 11.53 am	3 June, 11.41 pm
17 June	18 June, 12.37 am	3 July, 7.38 am
16 July	17 July, 2.31 pm	1 August, 2.31 pm
15 August	16 August, 5.38 am	30 August, 9.35 pm
13 September	14 September, 9.39 pm	29 September, 5.57 am
13 October	14 October, 1.55 pm	28 October, 4.24 pm
12 November	13 November, 4.27 am	27 November, 4.16 am
11 December	12 December, 6.32 pm	26 December, 7.33 pm

SPECIAL NOTES

- All times are local times for US Eastern Standard Time.
- Time is adjusted for daylight savings time when applicable. Please adjust for your state/country.
- Dates are based on the Gregorian calendar.

SPECIAL MOON EVENTS IN 2023

- Micro full moon: 6 January
- Super new moon: 21 January
- Micro full moon: 5 February
- Super new moon: 20 February
- Black moon: 19 May (*usually, each season has three months and three new moons; when a season has four new moons, the third new moon is called a black moon*)
- Super full moon: 1 August
- Micro new moon: 16 August
- Blue moon: 30 August
- Super full moon: 30 August
- Partial lunar eclipse visible in New York: 28 October

WHAT THE MOON PHASES MEAN

Every moon is a magical moon! Here is some useful information on what each moon phase means for us in terms of energy, as well as some suggestions on what to cast and when.

FULL

- The moon is full in the sky.
- Full energy! Big energy! Kapow!
- This moon gives you high-impact results, and is perfect for attraction spells of any type.
- It's a great time to explore and find your true path and purpose in life.
- Witches formally celebrate their relationship with the Divine once every 28 days during a full moon. This is called an 'esbat', literally a meeting with others in a coven or simply with the Divine.

WANING

- The moon is growing smaller in the sky. This occurs after the full moon and before the new moon.
- Energy is reduced.
- It's a good time to perform spells with a purpose and intention of getting rid of something that no longer serves you or to reduce an obstacle.
- It's a great time to give up a bad habit (*e.g. an addiction, a limiting or negative belief*).

DARK MOON

- No moon is visible in the sky.
- Traditionally, this is a time of introversion and rest.
- It's a good time for spells that ask for peace and creative flow.
- Experienced witches can use this moon for powerful healing through positive hexing.

NEW MOON

- This occurs the day after the dark moon and is good for fresh starts and renewal.
- Traditionally, it is the time to make seven wishes.
- It is a great time for spells of health and for the beginning of projects or businesses.
- A powerful time to cast spells for better mental health.

WAXING

- The moon is growing larger in the sky. This happens after the new moon and before the full moon.
- Energy is growing and expanding.
- It's a good time to perform spells with a purpose and intention of growth and moving towards something you desire.
- It's a powerful time to ask for more money, more positive relationships and better health.
- Wonderful for prosperity spells.
- Perfect for asking for bodily vitality, a pay rise, a new job, more recognition.

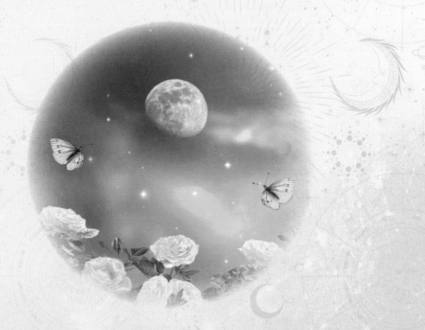

TIDES

Tides are, of course, linked to the moon. The rise and fall of the tides can be used as additional elements in your spells and aligning them with your spells can make them even more powerful. Being by the sea or water and seeing the tides ebb and flow always adds an extra dimension to your spell or ritual.

HIGH TIDE

- This tide brings things towards you, which is known for attraction.
- It's wonderful for prosperity spells.
- It's perfect for asking for better health, a pay rise, a new job, more recognition.

LOW TIDE

- This tide removes things, takes things away.
- It's perfect for removing obstacles, negative feelings, pain, bad memories, office politics.

KING TIDE

- These are very high and low tides that happen on a regular basis.
- On super full moons the tides are very extreme and are called king tides. Use these opportunities well! They are wonderful for calling in prosperity and business in particular.
- Energies are even more emphasised, so make sure what you are asking for is what you truly desire. It may be worth 'saving up' a desire especially for a king tide if it is a request that can wait.

OTHER TIMINGS

DAWN

- New beginnings
- New projects
- Creativity spells
- Initiations

SUNSET

- Completions
- Asking for help for a project or issue that may be long or difficult
- Spells for faith and preparation

MIDDAY

- Asking for increased personal power
- Asking for confidence and strength
- Asking for the courage to allow your 'light to shine'
- Worshipping during fire festivals such as Litha

MIDNIGHT

- ✦ The witching hour
- ✦ Asking for self-knowledge
- ✦ Asking for deep and lasting change
- ✦ Asking for help from our ancestors
- ✦ Turning dreams into reality

EQUINOX AND SOLSTICE TIMINGS – UNIVERSAL TIME (UTC)

- ✦ Spring equinox (Ostara) 20 March @ 21.24 UTC
- ✦ Summer solstice (Litha) 21 June @ 14.57 UTC
- ✦ Fall equinox (Mabon) 23 September @ 06.50 UTC
- ✦ Winter solstice (Yule) 22 December @ 03.27 UTC

EQUINOX AND SOLSTICE TIMINGS – NY, USA

- ✦ Spring equinox (Ostara) 20 March @ 5.24 pm EDT
- ✦ Summer solstice (Litha) 21 June @ 10.57 am EDT
- ✦ Fall equinox (Mabon) 23 September @ 2.50 am EDT
- ✦ Winter solstice (Yule) 21 December @ 10.27 am EST

ASTROLOGICAL CORRESPONDENCES FOR KEY MOON PHASES 2023

MONTH	ASTROLOGICAL SIGN	NEW MOON	FULL MOON
January	Cancer	–	6 January, 6.07 pm
	Capricorn	21 January, 3.53 pm	–
February	Leo	–	5 February, 1.28 pm
	Pisces	20 February, 2.05 am	–
March	Virgo	–	7 March, 7.40 am
	Pisces	21 March, 1.23 pm	–
April	Libra	–	6 April, 12.34 am
	Taurus	20 April, 12.12 am	–
May	Scorpio	–	5 May, 1.34 pm
	Taurus	19 May, 11.53 am	–
June	Sagittarius	–	3 June, 11.41 pm
	Cancer	18 June, 12.37 am	–
July	Capricorn	–	3 July, 7.38 am
	Cancer	17 July, 2.31 pm	–
August	Aquarius	–	1 August, 2.31 pm
	Leo	16 August, 5.38 am	–
	Pisces	–	30 August, 9.35 pm
September	Virgo	14 September, 9.39 pm	–
	Aries	–	29 September, 5.57 am
October	Libra	14 October, 1.55 pm	–
	Taurus	–	28 October, 4.24 pm
November	Scorpio	13 November, 4.27 am	–
	Gemini	–	27 November, 4.16 am
December	Sagittarius	12 December, 6.32 pm	–
	Cancer	–	26 December, 7.33 pm

WHAT DO THE ASTROLOGICAL SIGNS MEAN?

Separate to the meanings of the phases of the moon and the timings of the Wheel of the Year, there is also the layer of meaning often added where the moon is transiting within the signs of the zodiac. The moon makes a full transit of the earth (and the signs) every two and a half days.

I have listed below the astrological phases of the moon and some corresponding themes around which magical workings can be performed extra effectively.

CAPRICORN

Excellent for magic concerning planning, clarity, strategy, career and purpose, status, obstacle busting.

AQUARIUS

Excellent for magic concerning popularity, strengthening friendships, change, creativity, science, deepening spirituality and for the greater good.

PISCES

Great timing for magical workings concerning dreams, completion, increasing psychic ability and intuition, flow. Also a good time to do healing work around women's cycles.

ARIES

Great timing for magical workings concerning stamina, leadership, dealing with authority figures, strength, study.

TAURUS

Excellent for magic concerning family and children, love, home matters, purchase of real estate, creating sacred space in the home.

GEMINI

Great timing for magic concerning expansion, communication of all kinds, travel, writing, invocations.

CANCER

Great timing for magical workings concerning all kinds of emotional healing, cutting cords of old relationships. Great for healing the body, promoting health, particularly through diet.

LEO

Excellent for magical workings concerning self-esteem, personal power, status, authority of all kinds, improving relationship with boss.

Virgo

Great timing for workings concerning getting or keeping a job, exams, purification, clearing, detoxing of all kinds.

Libra

Excellent timing for magical workings concerning balance, justice, all legal matters, better health, weight balance.

Scorpio

Great timing for magical workings concerning all sexual matters, healing trauma, reducing gossip, increasing fun.

Sagittarius

Excellent timing for magical workings concerning truth, exposing dishonesty, clarity, and to ask for increased travel or protection during travel.

ELEMENTS AND DIRECTIONS

You might wish to utilise the elements and directions in your spells and workings to give yet another layer of powerful symbology and energy. Experienced witches use a compass (there is one within your mobile phone normally) if they are not sure of the directions when setting up a circle.

Here are some suggestions for ways of honouring each direction and corresponding element – but ultimately the combinations are up to you and certainly the geography around you. It used to be that there were very strict correspondences, usually highly influenced by the northern hemisphere, but now pagans and witches all over the world combine the elements and directions in the way that the geography in front of them most calls for. So, for example, if you were standing facing east in Sydney, Australia the dominant element in the environment would be the ocean (water) and so I cast east as water.

EARTH – NORTH

- Salt, earth, oils such as oak moss, patchouli
- Standing on earth, sprinkling of earth and salt, anointing stones
- Represents resilience, order, law, politics, education, security, money
- Green/brown
- Night

FIRE – SOUTH

- Candles, open flames of any kind, oils such as pepper, ginger, frankincense
- Lighting flame, passing flame around the circle, anointing with oil
- Represents passion, purpose, strength, achievement, destruction of what is not needed
- Masculine – sun
- Red
- Noon

AIR – EAST

- Incense, fragrance, smoke, kites, balloons, oils such as bergamot, lime, eucalyptus
- Smudging, blowing smoke, bubbles, bells, singing bowls
- Represents communication, creativity, logic, travel, new beginnings, ideas, flow
- Yellow
- Dawn

WATER – WEST

- Salt water, moon water, shells, rain, oils such as rose, ylang ylang
- Anointing with water, passing the cup
- Relationships, love, psychic connection, birth/death/rebirth
- Represents relationships, love, psychic connection, birth/death/rebirth
- Feminine – moon
- Blue

WHEEL OF THE YEAR

As the path of the witch is an earth-based faith, the witches' sabbats, or 'holidays', are intrinsically connected to the cycles of nature. Primarily, the themes of birth, death and rebirth are played out across a year that is divided into light and dark, male and female, sun and moon, growth and rest and heat and cold.

Traditionally, most of the celebrations were linked to the cycles of the northern hemisphere, so witches in the southern hemisphere 'flip the year' around to suit their seasons.

Importantly, these sacred times connect you with the light and land, and with the seasons. The land is our mother; she feeds us, shelters us and gives us comfort and joy. The festivals give us a chance to give something back to her and honour all that she does. As modern people we often forget this and feel disconnected without quite knowing why.

The continuous cycle lends itself to the image of a wheel as you can see. The ancient Celts and their predecessors saw time as a wheel or spiral divided by eight festivals as follows. Modern witches can use the 'themes' of each celebration to do magical workings of their own in complete synergy with the natural cycles. The dates featured on solstices/equinoxes are to be used as a guide only, so please refer to the diary itself for accuracy.

PLEASE NOTE: where these festivals fall within the calendar spreads within this diary, I have given further information on the festival and some suggestions on how to celebrate the Sabbath with meaning.

SAMHAIN (HALLOWE'EN)

- Southern, 30 April; northern, 31 October
- Celebration of death as a continuation of life
- Borders between the dead and living are not fixed and impassable
- The veil between the worlds are at their thinnest so one can ask the ancestors and spirits for guidance and communication on the future
- Celebrating where you came from – ancestral energy
- Traditional time for scrying
- Witches' New Year!

YULE (WINTER SOLSTICE)

- Southern, 21–23 June; northern, 21–23 December
- Longest night of the year
- Mid-winter festival linked to the Christian Christmas
- Archetypally linked with the birth of a child of promise and light: Dionysus, Arthur, Jesus, Baldur
- Celebrates the return of the sun and thus hope
- Abundance spells and charms
- Giving thanks and gifts of goodwill

IMBOLC (CANDLEMAS)

- Southern, 1 August; northern, 1 February
- Celebration of light returning
- Goddess as Brigid (St Brigid)
- Fire festival
- Clarity and healing
- Light to shine, self-knowledge/creation

OSTARA (SPRING EQUINOX)

- Southern, 21–23 September; northern, 21–23 March
- Night and day are equal, but moving towards summer
- Balance and growth
- Leave what you don't want and create the new
- Fertility and love
- New projects

BELTANE (MAY DAY)

- Southern, 31 October/1 November; northern, 30 April/1 May
- Marriage of the goddess and the god
- Maypoles – phallic and yonic symbolism
- Love magic and fertility (weddings/handfastings)
- Masculine and feminine balance

LITHA (SUMMER SOLSTICE)

- Southern, 21–23 December; northern, 21–23 June
- Longest day, shortest night
- Sun is at its fullest power yet year begins to wane from here
- What brings light and joy into your life – develop this
- Self-development
- Celebration of the masculine divine

LAMMAS (LUGHNASADH)

- Southern, 1 February; northern, 1 August
- First harvest – first loaf baked
- The god begins his journey into the underworld
- Sorrow and celebration
- Fruition, taking stock and harvesting what you have achieved

MABON (AUTUMN EQUINOX)

- Southern, 21–22 March; northern, 21–22 September
- Harvesting the main crop
- Take stock of what has served you well, and what has not
- What needs repairing before the dark comes
- Preparation for harder times

THE MOON AND OUR BODY

We are moon-influenced animals, even if most of us don't go howling under it! Within long-held knowledge, there are a number of ways that it's believed the moon impacts our physical bodies.

DETOXING

Many of us at some stage feel the need to re-energise the body through a detox of some sort. Usually it's after a period of overindulgence: perhaps too much rich food, alcohol or sugar. Detoxes have become quite fashionable and all kinds of weird and wacky systems and products are now being promoted. I am not a big fan of detoxing in its newest, most faddish form, but if a detox to you means a period of consuming more deeply nourishing food in smaller quantities, less stimulants and alcohol and more sleep, I am all for it!

Should you decide a detox is something you do wish to undertake, the moon can help you make this time more successful.

One-day detoxes: early on the day before a new moon (dark moon), set an intention over the next 24 hours to release what your body does not need. Upon waking on the new moon day, set an intention to release all that you don't need and start your detox.

Longer detoxes: begin your program on a full moon, setting an intention that as the moon wanes so will the toxins be released from your body. Continue your program during the waning period but no longer.

Note: unless you are sure you are fit enough to embark on a detox program, do not attempt to do it yourself. Seek professional advice.

HAIR

I know many of you lunar-tics love cutting and growing your hair by the moon cycles and I know that full and new moon days are some of the most popular days for hairdressers all over the world! It is thought that different phases influence hair growth just like they influence tides, so it's no surprise that full and waxing moons are best friends to those of us who want longer locks!

Growing your hair: traditionally, should you wish to grow your hair only cut it when it is in its most active phase during the full or waxing moon.

Keeping it similar length: if you wish to preserve your haircut (very handy for those who have a fringe or short hair), cut your hair on a waning moon.

Strengthening: for giving your hair treatment days, you might try new moon days and waxing moons. For the mother of all good hair days, go for the full moon in Cancer for all your conditioning and cutting treatments.

For hair removal: whether you wax, laser or shave, the best time to take that hair off is in the waning moon cycle. It will stay away longer.

WEIGHT BALANCE

In ethical witchcraft we don't talk about losing weight. Instead, it's about having the body reaching a healthy balance. Setting your intention and beginning on the full moon is a great idea. This gets the mind used to the idea that this is a great idea and something you want. You might even cast a spell for health and vitality that night to boost it along. There is a good one free on my site **www.themodernwitch.com.**

Waning moon: begin your program straight after a full moon and notice that the moon is waning, taking with it extra weight and fluid. You will lose more weight more rapidly during a waning moon if this is what you seek.

New moon: when the moon reaches a new moon phase we again do a ritual to boost our intention. Lighting a candle and simply asking the universe to continue to assist you to reach your goal and to achieve greater health is enough.

Waxing moon: we must be careful here not to eat foods that are not aligned with our intention, as waxing moon cycles will hold them to the body far more than during waning cycles. However, we generally have more energy during waxing moons so this is the time to boost your activity levels and burn off what you consume more easily.

Back to full moon: be grateful for what you have achieved (or achieved so far) and set your intention moving forward. We express love and admiration for what our body is and does.

BALANCING YOUR BODY WITH THE MOON

There is some excellent research available on the correlation of lunar light, moon phase and bodily biorhythms like those related to our hormonal and fertility cycles. There seem to be two camps on this: the first that sees no correlation with the moon cycles of 28–29 days with the typical female cycle of the same length or with a spike in fertility around the full moon, and the second camp that recognises this long-held wisdom as fact.

If you are female and you have a menstrual cycle that is radically less than or more than 29 days, you may consider it beneficial to balance your cycle. One way that seems to work is to literally watch the moon for five minutes each night. We need light to activate a whole cascade of bodily functions and it seems the fertility cycle is but one. If you wish you could visualise your most fertile time at a full moon (full power!) and your wise blood flowing around a dark/new moon (letting go, starting afresh).

THE LUNAR RETURN

Across a number of ancient cultures such as the Egyptian and Sumerian, it was believed that the moon phase upon birth triggered the beginning of life and remained as a person's peak time energetically throughout life. This was especially evident for women as it determined her most fertile time. Records of Sumerian medicine indicated a belief that a woman was most fertile when the moon was at the same phase as her birth. Ancient Celts and Egyptians recorded the moon phase at birth and told both sexes when they came of age. We call this a lunar return.

A lunar return is not what astrological moon sign you were born in – it's more astronomy than astrology! Rather, it's what actual phase was in the sky upon your birth e.g. full moon, quarter moon, two days before new moon etc.

So, the simple idea of knowing which phase of the moon you were born on and noting it, as well as keeping an eye on the moon regularly, seems to induce more hormonal balance in both sexes.

It is also the peak time of performance for mental and physical energy. Knowing when you will be feeling most vital and energetic really does have profound impacts in everyday life! Knowing when you are at the top of your game for sport, exams or decision making is an advantage. Knowing when you may not have a lot of energy (the opposite of your lunar return moon) is also valuable to know.

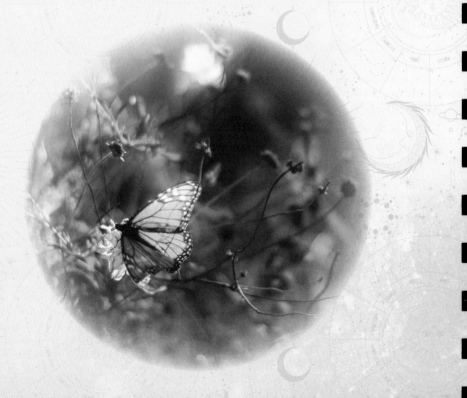

DEITIES OF THE MOON

One of the aspects of lunar lore that I fell in love with pretty quicky as a young person was that of the gods and goddesses. I loved mythos (the stories with a truth) even as a child. Yet as I grew I began to understand that these stories and art weren't just little fairytales like the 'man in the moon', but they were so much deeper and more instructive than that. These deities could help me transform myself and flow forward just like the moon phases did. These amazing queens, goddesses, gods and kings led by example and, boy, don't we all need good strong examples.

Witches believe that we each have a spark of the goddess and god within us. In natural reciprocity, the goddess and god have a spark of us within them. Knowing intimately that by having a spark of divinity within you, you are indeed goddess or god, this tends to change reality for you. It is difficult to experience self-hate if you know that you have the Divine within you. Self-esteem comes flowing back, flooding us with positive change if we truly come to this realisation.

Here are some deities I recommend working with that have links to the moon:

Artemis (Greek)

Aradia (Roman)

Arianrhod (Welsh)

Brigid (Celtic)

Cerridwen (Welsh)

Circe (Greek)

Diana (Roman)

Freyja (Norse)

Hina (Polynesian)

Hekate (Greek)

Mani (Norse)

Morgan Le Fay (Celtic)

Skadi (Norse)

Thoth (Egyptian)

Triple Goddess (archetype, European Wiccan)

Yemaya (Yorbian)

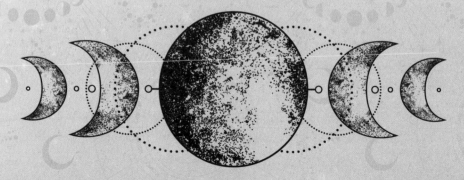

LUNAR ENERGIES
AND CRYSTALS

Utilising crystals to focus and capture energy is something that many practitioners, both pagan and non-pagan, do. One of the most popular ways of cleansing and charging your crystals is to place them under the moonlight. However, there are some subtle ways of enhancing the energies of crystals by matching the specific lunar energy at certain times in the cycle or using solar energy instead.

LUNAR ENERGIES

Cleansing: leave your crystals out under the power of a full moon or waxing moon. If you are using the powers of the waxing moon, leave the crystals out on multiple nights right up to full moon.

Dedicating for matters of prosperity: I have had success with leaving crystals in a bowl of shallow water out in the moonlight. The water promotes the flow of money towards you.

Dedicating for matters of growth: place crystals on living soil or plants. Grass is perfect, as is a healthy pot plant. Leave out under moonlight and then leave out for a full day of sunshine too.

Dedicating to absorb negative energies: many crystals are useful to us in the way that they help us dispel or absorb negative energies. Jet, obsidian, black tourmaline and pink kunzite are good examples of this. Give these crystals an extra boost by dedicating them or charging them on a dark or waning moon cycle.

Dedicating for meditation or channelling: I very much like to dedicate stones such as lapis, amethyst, clear quartz or turquoise during dark moons when the energies are aligned for more introverted, inward-facing activities. I like to take these crystals into the darker parts of my garden or even areas shaded slightly by rocks but still able to be graced by the sky. I try and retrieve them just before dawn to keep the integrity of the 'darkness' intact.

SOLAR ENERGIES

While I love to leave my crystals out basking in the silvery moonlight, there are some crystals that thrive under the fiery sun. I find that naturally gold or warm-coloured stones such as amber and citrine often need a good dose of solar energy to keep them 'happy', so don't be afraid to do so. When dedicating your crystals, you will still need to cleanse them first in whichever manner works best for you, but here are some charging and dedication suggestions using solar energies that work for me.

Dedicating for health: on three days running from dawn til dusk leave out your crystals that will be dedicated to health and healing. Mid-summer is an ideal time to do this, as is the time around the new moon.

Dedicating for inspiration: get a boost from the biggest fire of all to fan your personal fires of inspiration, the sun. Place your stones on a natural surface like grass or a plant and leave out from dawn til dusk for seven days. Springtime is a great time to do this each year.

Gifts: when I am giving a crystal to a man, I always leave it out under the sun for a day or so. The sun gives the stone a charging of masculine energy, which I believe enables it to bind more quickly to its new owner. For women, leave under the moon instead.

CRYSTALS FOR MOON PHASES

Here is a list of the crystals I find really compatible and powerful with particular moon phases. You can use them in gridding or mandala, on your altar, to boost spells and for energy raising, and you can wear them, carry them or pop them in a juju bag. Stones that are great universals with lunar energy include clear quartz, Herkimer diamonds and diamonds. You can also use metals such as platinum and silver. And pearls, being from the ocean, are also very compatible with lunar workings.

Dark moon: jet

New moon: celestine

Waxing crescent 1: aventurine

Waxing crescent 2: lepidolite

Waxing crescent 3: charoite

Waxing crescent 4: rose quartz

Waxing crescent 5: emerald

Waxing crescent 6: pyrite

First quarter moon: azurite

Waxing gibbous 1: yellow jasper

Waxing gibbous 2: aquamarine

Waxing gibbous 3: obsidian

Waxing gibbous 4: hematite

Waxing gibbous 5: carnelian

Waxing gibbous 6: rhodonite

Full moon: moonstone

Waning gibbous 1: tiger's eye

Waning gibbous 2: turquoise

Waning gibbous 3: bloodstone

Waning gibbous 4: larimar

Waning gibbous 5: azurite

Waning gibbous 6: fluorite

Last quarter moon: ocean jasper

Waning crescent 1: black tourmaline

Waning crescent 2: red jasper

Waning crescent 3: orange calcite

Waning crescent 4: smokey quartz

Waning crescent 5: amethyst

THE MOON AND PLANTS

For millennia, people all over the planet have been farming and gardening by the moon cycles. It is believed that because the earth operates under a gravity field that is influenced by the moon (and less by other planets), this affects the growth of plants. Just as we can see the moon's influence on the ocean and other bodies of water, it is believed that the moon changes the level of water in the soil, affecting seedling and plant growth.

There are amazing farmer's almanacs you can buy for your region each year that give very detailed planting suggestions and harvesting recommendations, all guided by the moon and astrological information (check the Resources section at the end of the book for details). While this isn't a gardening diary, I have added some suggestions and it certainly is worth mentioning here the basic lunar rules of thumb when it comes to gardening by the moon. As more and more of us choose to grow our own organic herbs, vegies and other plants, knowing how the moon may influence your patch may make the difference between a fair, good or bumper crop.

FULL MOON

As the water rises and swells within the soil, this is a perfect time to plant seeds. It is also a good time to harvest some plants at the peak of their goodness.

WANING

As the water level sinks, it's time for planting your below-ground plants such as potatoes, carrots, onions, parsnips and beetroot.

NEW MOON

Growth slows. Prune, trim and fertilise. Apply any necessary natural pest control. Weed.

WAXING

Growth time again. Water begins to rise. A good time for planting your above-ground crops such as pumpkin, tomatoes, cauliflower, kale, lettuce and spinach.

'FERTILE' ZODIAC SIGNS

Water and earth signs are considered the 'growth' times for plants. When the moon enters these signs, it's a fine time to plant or prune back for growth.

'BARREN' ZODIAC SIGNS

All your maintenance chores should be done on the times when the moon is in fire and air signs.

Learn more in my book *The Enchanted Moon.*

POSITIVE BEGINNINGS

This section is about learning how to ask for and get what you really want.

There are a lot of people who have decided they won't even try for new year's intentions anymore because they can never keep them. Yes, we know that some people set unreasonable goals (lose huge amounts of weight in one month anyone?), but it seems that the big reason we don't achieve what we say we want is that, really, we don't want it all that badly.

'I do want it though!' you might say. 'But I really do want to get healthy or I really do want that new car/house/job/love!' Here is the big reason why you may not want it all that much – because right now, it either doesn't align with your values or you are wanting goals that actually belong to someone else. You simply aren't that devoted or you get distracted.

Then for some there is the feeling of 'What if I get this thing, what then?' Will my family still love me? Will this new job actually really be better? Will my life change so much that I can't control it anymore?

Now take all of that and look at it. Feel it. And you know – that smells like confusion and fear to me!

So what I have done to assist you to get clearer about what you really want is an exercise I get participants in my infamous new year's workshops to do (see later in this diary). Fill this out before you do any new year's spells or rituals, and I think you may find you get a big truth bomb hitting you in a very good way. You'll sort out what matters to you – really – and you can base your resolutions on that. And then you can be devoted to what you want to be, rather than what you might be unconsciously doing. You will be able to track your progress and update it as you grow each month on the monthly header pages in this book.

For me, I love the gateway of new year (which we will undergo in the upcoming pages) because it is certainly a gateway into a new and fresh start if we wish it to be so. It's a kind of catalyst for change. Many ancient cultures saw the beginning of a new year as an opportunity to journey through a gateway into something new, but to do so meant a kind of leap of faith, both literally and figuratively.

The Romans, for example, took this idea literally, creating new year's doorways dedicated to the goddess Jana and the god Janus, where the people jumped though from one side to another to signify that they had indeed left the energy of the previous year behind and accepted fully a new start. The Mayans smashed statues within gateways representing the old year when that one was up, and you had to walk over the rubble to get to the 'new year' gateway.

Yes, we can all jump though a new gateway. We can all be brave and courageous and inspired. We all can be the leaders and heroes and happy endings in own story. So let us begin . . .

GETTING CLEAR
ABOUT 2023

Here are some great questions to ask yourself to get clear about what you want for 2023:

+ What are my values? (Values are guiding ideals and principles e.g. honesty, compassion, creativity, calmness, fairness, independence, freedom.)

_____

+ What are my needs? (Needs are things you must have to be at your best.)

_____

+ What am I devoted to right now? (You can be devoted to things that are positive or not so positive. You are devoted to what you actually do e.g. if you eat a lot of potato chips then you are devoted to eating potato chips.)

_____

+ What do I want to be devoted to?

_____

+ Take those values and needs and think about what would give you the greatest pleasure in 2023.

_____

Now, let's get even clearer by discerning even further based on your values and real pleasures . . .

+ What would I definitely wish to leave behind in 2023 (e.g. old patterns, negative experiences, bad habits, body inbalances)?

_____

+ Based on my values and pleasures, what would I love to experience but haven't as yet?

_____

- If I could make one positive intention for the community or planet as a whole it would be:

  _____

- Taking all this into consideration, the new year's intentions I would love to set are:

  _____

- My biggest action steps for the months of 2023:

January: _____

February: _____

March: _____

April: _____

May: _____

June: _____

July: _____

August: _____

September: _____

October: _____

November: _____

December: _____

NEW YEAR'S GATEWAY JUMP

Like the ancient Romans, I love a good new year's gateway jump! Every year I start the year this way, and I know many of you have gotten on board with this ritual now and do it every year too. The ancient Romans obviously enjoyed leaping through the gateway of the new year with goddess Jana and god Janus, who face backwards and forwards at the same time.

This is a fun ritual to do alone or with friends and it features the gateway deities Jana and Janus (January was named after them). There are lots of versions of this little ritual but all of them involve a physical jump, which I think kickstarts our mind and spirit too.

GATEWAY RITUAL

AHEAD OF TIME, FIND A GATEWAY TO JUMP THOUGH — DOORWAYS OR GATES ARE PERFECT, OR YOU CAN EVEN CREATE YOUR OWN BY STRETCHING SOME PRETTY FABRIC BETWEEN TWO TREES AT LEAST A METRE ABOVE HEAD LEVEL OR PLACING A BROOM ON THE FLOOR AND LEAPING OVER IT.

Gather: incense for burning • a gift for the genus loci *(the friendly spirits of the place)* • a piece of chalk or a ribbon or broom to mark the gateway jump • a silver candle and a gold candle • a bowl of water with two handfuls of salt added • your list of intentions for the new year of 2023.

Go to where you are going to do the new year jump. Burn your incense in a bowl and allow the smoke to purify the area. You might thank the genus loci for their help and leave a little gift.

When you are done, draw a line with the chalk or place the ribbon across the ground of the threshold of the gateway or doorway.

Light the silver candle and say:

'Jana of the gateway! Goddess of what was and what will be! I am ready to step through 2022 into the sparkling new possibility of 2023. I have thought about my desires and wish you to grant my intentions if they be for the good of all!'

Light the gold candle and say:

'Janus of the gateway! You are the god of what is behind me and what is in front of me! I am ready to leap excitedly into the future of 2023. Help me achieve my intentions and so much more if it be for the good of all!'

Now, place your hands in the bowl of salted water and say:

'In your presence, I clear away any burdens or poor actions. I cleanse away my fears, doubts and any obstacles in the way of this, a new year!'

Wash your hands, imagining all negative things in your life being cleansed.

Read out your intentions for 2023 three times. Be excited about these intentions. Don't be shy about them! Feel that excitement ripple right through your body.

Step towards the gateway or threshold, saying in a clear voice:

'Jana and Janus, take me through the gateway easily and with your protection! I step forward into the new!'

Now, step or jump confidently forward through the gateway.

Say:

'Thank you! Yes!'

And clap three times loudly.

Thank Janus and Jana and ask:

'What do I do next?'

Listen for any messages or ideas. Act upon these as soon as you can.

Blow out the candles after midnight if possible.

Throw the salted water down the drain.

Happy New Year, fellow jumpers!

JANUARY

- What would I like to create, experience and manifest this month?

Space for myself -
Self-care; down time
Flow, calm, AWARE

- What are the important dates for me this month?

- What would give me joy this month?

Honing a skill

- What am I devoted to?

The liminal space - the space
between - awareness

- Ideas, musings, actions:

TA'AROA

GOD OF THE MONTH — JANUARY

A new year gives us a kind of psychological push towards the new. I see '1 January' on a calendar and often I'm excited about the next 365 days and what I might be able to create into them.

It seems then that a deity of creation is perfect to start our new year off with because they, too, are often creating into the void, a place of pure possibility, and starting things anew.

Ta'aroa is the Tahitian god who creates all things. In the beginning there is an empty nothingness, and it is only he who exists cocooned within a smooth white egg. Ta'aroa travels through this space and considers how things are and wills for more within his current existence.

At this, he cracks open his shell and finds himself in this dark space of nothingness. No stars, no earth, no sound, no smells; just he.

He breaks the shell completely and takes the pieces to create the rocks and sand and soil, forming it into a ball. He curls over and his backbone forms the mighty mountains. His joyful tears pool into lakes, rivers, rain and the ocean itself. With his own feathers he creates the birds; with his fingernails, the scales on reptiles and fish and the shells of turtles. He allows his blood to spill a little and it forms rainbows in the sky. His breath forms the winds.

From the clay, he fashions and creates other creators. He creates the first god Tāne. Then Hina, Ru, Maui, Lono and many, many others. All have their realms and Tāne hangs the moon and creates the sun and stars so there is a sky.

The earth, Tumi-Nui, then is fully created and Ta'aroa decides to create the being of man. Man is created and quickly multiplied, delighting Ta'aroa. Man then creates too, raising himself from the clay and travelling through the levels of the earth, being innovative, having ideas, creating over and over again.

SPELL FOR CREATION

THIS IS A BEAUTIFUL AND HOPEFUL SPELL TO DO IN NATURE IF POSSIBLE.
NEW MOON IS A GREAT TIME TO CAST BUT ANY MOON IS MAGICAL!

Gather: a fresh egg • textas • a place in the garden to dig a small hole or a pot with soil • a white or green candle • a small bowl of aqua luna *(this is water left out under a full moon for blessing)* • flowers.

Ahead of time take the egg, handling it carefully. Grab the textas and write the things you most want to create for this year on the egg shell. You can write words or draw symbols; it is up to you.

Go to the place in your garden/outdoors you have chosen and light the candle. Put a flower in your hair or behind one ear.

TAKE A BREATH. CLOSE YOUR EYES IF YOU LIKE, AND SAY:

'Creator of all things, Ta'aroa, I humbly call you and ask you to help me create a year to remember for myself.'

OFFER SOME FLOWERS TO TA'AROA, PLACING THEM ON THE GROUND. SAY:

'As you created all things allow me to break out of my current state and create anew.'

CRACK OPEN THE EGG IN THE HOLE IN THE GROUND OR THE SOIL IN THE POT.

IMAGINE NOW THAT GROWTH AND MOMENTUM BEGINS
TOWARDS EVERYTHING YOU HAVE ASKED FOR.

COVER UP THE EGG WITH THE SOIL. TAKE YOUR AQUA LUNA
AND POUR A LITTLE ON THE SOIL WITH EGG AND SAY:

'It is here that it begins.'

BLOW OUT THE CANDLE WITH THANKS. PARTICIPATE
TOWARDS YOUR CREATIVE GOALS.

26 Monday ◑

Waxing

Boxing Day.

27 Tuesday ◑

Waxing

There are a few good days around this time to remove any unwanted hair as it will grow back more slowly.

28 Wednesday ◑

Waxing

29 Thursday ◑

Waxing

DECEMBER

30 Friday ◑

Waxing

31 Saturday ◑

Waxing

New Year's Eve spell: set your intentions for 2023 if you haven't already! Do the ritual with Jana and Janus of the gateway or mark the end of this year with a small ritual of gratitude before you go out to celebrate. Just a simple candle lit with intention and a special honouring of all the energies or deities that assisted you this year is a great start.

1 Sunday ◑   January 2023

Waxing

Welcome to a new year!

Catch the wave of global 'fresh start, new beginnings' energy . . . release your intentions today!

DECEMBER							JANUARY						
M	T	W	T	F	S	S	M	T	W	T	F	S	S
				1	2	3	4						1
5	6	7	8	9	10	11	2	3	4	5	6	7	8
12	13	14	15	16	17	18	9	10	11	12	13	14	15
19	20	21	22	23	24	25	16	17	18	19	20	21	22
26	**27**	**28**	**29**	**30**	**31**		23	24	25	26	27	28	29
							30	31					

2 Monday ◐

Waxing

3 Tuesday ◐

Waxing

4 Wednesday ◐

Waxing

5 Thursday ◐

Waxing

6 Friday

Waxing

Friday was named after the Norse goddess of love, war and magic, Freyja.

7 Saturday ○ Full moon in Cancer 6.07 pm EST

Micro full moon

Start the year with confidence and allow yourself to enjoy new experiences and ways of doing things. Set intentions for the success of your business or work life.

8 Sunday ◑

Waning

Joyfully flow forward without fear in my name.

– THE GODDESS

JANUARY

M	T	W	T	F	S	S
						1
2	3	4	5	6	7	8
9	10	11	12	13	14	15
16	17	18	19	20	21	22
23	24	25	26	27	28	29
30	31					

9 Monday ☽

Waning

10 Tuesday ☽

Waning

11 Wednesday ☽

Waning

12 Thursday ☽

Waning

13 Friday ☽

Waning

14 Saturday ☽

Waning

15 Sunday ☽

Waning

JANUARY

M	T	W	T	F	S	S
						1
2	3	4	5	6	7	8
9	**10**	**11**	**12**	**13**	**14**	**15**
16	17	18	19	20	21	22
23	24	25	26	27	28	29
30	31					

16 Monday ◑

Waning

17 Tuesday ◑

Waning

18 Wednesday ◑

Waning

19 Thursday ◑

Waning

20 Friday

Dark moon

Relax, go within, let go of anything that is keeping you stuck.

21 Saturday ☽ New moon in Capricorn 3.53 pm EST

Super new moon

A moon to inspire fresh things and a new take on things. Plan the next few months if you can because it's a super powerful new moon!

22 Sunday ◐

Waxing

JANUARY

M	T	W	T	F	S	S
						1
2	3	4	5	6	7	8
9	10	11	12	13	14	15
16	**17**	**18**	**19**	**20**	**21**	**22**
23	24	25	26	27	28	29
30	31					

23 Monday ☽

Waxing

24 Tuesday ☽

Waxing

25 Wednesday ☽

Waxing

26 Thursday ☽

Waxing

27 Friday ☽

Waxing

28 Saturday ☽

Waxing

29 Sunday ☽

Waxing

How are those new year's intentions going?

Delight in the song of new beginnings.

- THE GODDESS

JANUARY

M	T	W	T	F	S	S
						1
2	3	4	5	6	7	8
9	10	11	12	13	14	15
16	17	18	19	20	21	22
23	**24**	**25**	**26**	**27**	**28**	**29**
30	31					

FEBRUARY

• What would I like to create, experience and manifest this month?

Improve my knitting

• What are the important dates for me this month?

• What would give me joy this month?

Stillness, calm, flow

• What am I devoted to?

Self-care,

• Ideas, musings, actions:

AENGUS

GOD OF THE MONTH – FEBRUARY

Aengus falls in love with a girl he first sees in his dreams.

No ordinary man, Aengus is a handsome god from the mythos of Ireland and Scotland. The son of the most powerful of the gods from these cultures, the Dagda and the river queen Boann, he is young, beautiful, blue eyed and fair. He is considered a healer of broken things, a god of spring and high summer and one who represents true love.

This dream is incredibly vivid and he becomes obsessed with finding this lovely woman. He asks his mother Boann and the cow goddess of the Milky Way, Bealach na Bó Finne, to help him locate her. Both goddesses search far and wide. Aengus also gets his father involved. The Dagda asks King Bodb Derg to also assist, and it is he who finds the elusive girl at the lake at Dragon's Mouth another year later.

Aengus arrives and is horrified to find the girl of his dreams, Caer Ibormeith, among 150 girls chained in pairs. He is told that the girls are enchanted and that every second Samhain the girls turn into swans for a year and are free at this time. Caer tells him that if he can identify her in her swan form, out of all the other swans, he can marry her.

And so he waits, and on Samhain all the girls shrug off their human form along with their chains and transform into swans. Aengus knows which swan is his beloved and turns himself into a swan too. They fly away together and sing a haunting song that puts to sleep anyone who hears it. The enchantment is broken and they are together always.

While this is a highly romantic story, it does have some lessons for us about self-doubt, patience and the shadow side of love if we look deeply.

Ritual for love of all kinds

This spell should ideally be cast on a new moon, but every moon is magical for love. Please remember, if you are casting for romantic love, ensure you do not cast for a particular person. This goes against free will and is unethical.

Gather: two gold or white candles • two feathers – *any kind, but if you are near a place where swans live, gather some shed feathers.*

Ahead of time, consider where you would like to receive more love e.g. the attraction of a partner, friendships, towards yourself, the healing of someone or an animal that has experienced a lack of love.

Open a circle if you wish. Light the first candle and say:

'Sweet Aengus, god of love, son of the Dagna, I ask that you pave the way for love in my life.'

State out loud exactly what kind of love you are asking for.

Hold the feathers in your hand. Close your eyes, pull up energy from the earth, and as you breathe in, take in love from the whole planet. Allow yourself to experience the emotion clearly. Allow it to spread into every cell. Take your time. Then hold the two feathers in your hand.

Allow the love to charge up the feathers and say:

'Please accept my offering in honour of you and your love, Caer.'

Let the feathers go. They may simply fall or fly away in the wind.

Light the second candle and say:

'I extend this great love to myself, others and the world.'

Express your thanks and think about one step forward you can take.

Blow out both candles when you are ready.

WHEEL OF THE YEAR

Imbolc

1 February

You just know things have changed when spring is working its way back into the earth. The mornings are warmer – a miracle! It's not so hard to get out of bed. The light changes. The birds get more active. The sunlight feels stronger on our skin and that feels good! I call this awakening of spring the 'sacred shake'. It's like the earth itself has cracked that icy skin and is having a big stretch. More energy from the earth means more energy for us. We are again in a transition season and one that is leading us towards growth, warmth, fecundity and momentum.

Imbolc is a festival that allows us to celebrate the returning of the light after the darkness of winter. It is an ancient Celtic festival and has its origins in a spring celebration honouring the goddess Brigid in her fire aspect. This beginning of the change of season was considered to be the time that Brigid's fire sparks again and awakens the earth. It is said, as she walked the fields, she brought life back to the land, melted the ice and gave fertility to the animals.

So what does this all mean for us modern folk? I take the timing of Imbolc as a little nudge to change my focus from introversion to gentle action. I alter my diet to a spring seasonal one. I try and get outside more and observe the birds and animals so busy at this time. I do workings for love, prosperity and more happiness. All this new energy, this aligning with the season, makes life lighter and more enjoyable.

HOW TO CELEBRATE IMBOLC

First, an Imbolc altar is one of the joys of the year! I take the opportunity before Imbolc to clear everything off my altar and give it a good spring clean. I prepare fragrant flower waters of rose and mint and have everything sparkling clean. Then I create a spring altar of flowers, herbs, cakes and pretty candles and do a ritual honouring the rites of spring and the goddess Brigid in particular.

Perhaps I might make the traditional 'Brigid's Cross' from straw or twigs from the garden. This is fun to do with your kids, and there are good tutorials on the internet.

Second, as Brigid is the bringer of fire as well as the goddess of water sources such as wells, we know it is she who can transform water into something sacred. So if you leave out an offering for Brigid – I like to leave out some honey and milk, or cakes along with a bowl of water – it is said that she will at dawn accept your beautiful offering and bless the water. The water is special then, as it is the very essence of regeneration and rebirth. You can drink the water for health and vitality or bathe in it, or as the old stories go, rub some on your face and you won't age another year!

30 Monday ◑

Waxing

Cwood mtg 1 - 3pm

31 Tuesday ◑

Waxing

May Brigid's blessings be upon you. It is the Festival of Imbolc tomorrow. Leave out a bowl of water for Brigid to bless for your health and beauty.

Krings delivery 9am

1 Wednesday ◑

Waxing

Imbolc – the light returns to the land. May the blessings of Brigid be upon you! If you have collected it, use the goddess Brigid's Imbolc healing waters to drink or for your potions.

2 Thursday ◑

Waxing

Krings / Stoneback 830am

3 Friday ◑

Waxing

Krings /Stoneback 8.30am
- dwasher install

4 Saturday ◑

Waxing

If you wish to grow your hair, this is a great time to trim it to promote growth.

5 Sunday ○ Full moon in Leo 1.28 pm EST

Micro full moon

A no BS full moon where this big energy can get you what you want. Choose carefully, queens and kings!

| JANUARY | | | | | | | | FEBRUARY | | | | | | |
M	T	W	T	F	S	S		M	T	W	T	F	S	S
						1			1	2	3	4	5	
2	3	4	5	6	7	8		6	7	8	9	10	11	12
9	10	11	12	13	14	15		13	14	15	16	17	18	19
16	17	18	19	20	21	22		20	21	22	23	24	25	26
23	24	25	26	27	28	29		27	28					
30	31													

6 Monday ◗

Waning

7 Tuesday ◗

Waning

8 Wednesday ◗

Waning

9 Thursday ◗

Waning

10 Friday ◗

Waning

11 Saturday ◗

Waning

12 Sunday ◗

Waning

Delight in your gifts, for they are yours
Wrapped in your Self and no other.

– THE GODDESS

M	T	W	T	F	S	S
		1	2	3	4	5
6	7	8	9	10	11	12
13	14	15	16	17	18	19
20	21	22	23	24	25	26
27	28					

FEBRUARY

13 Monday

Waning

14 Tuesday

Waning

Happy Lupercalia! (Valentine's Day)

The ancient Roman festival of Lupercalia celebrated virility, wildness, fertility and lust! Today, ride the energetic wave of love of what is now called Valentine's Day and cast a love spell to improve your current relationship or to attract a new one that suits you perfectly.

15 Wednesday

Waning

16 Thursday

Waning

17 Friday ◑

Waning

18 Saturday ◑

Waning

19 Sunday ●

Dark moon

A sacred night to release trauma.

FEBRUARY

M	T	W	T	F	S	S
		1	2	3	4	5
6	7	8	9	10	11	12
13	**14**	**15**	**16**	**17**	**18**	**19**
20	21	22	23	24	25	26
27	28					

20 Monday ☽ New moon in Pisces 2.05 am EST

Super new moon

A dreamy, deep new moon that gently invites us towards emotional harmony.

21 Tuesday ◐

Waxing

22 Wednesday ◐

Waxing

23 Thursday ◐

Waxing

24 Friday ◑

Waxing

25 Saturday ◑

Waxing

26 Sunday ◑

Waxing

Listen not to the crowd around you
When it comes to your worth,
Instead love comes first from the inside out
From the glowing flame of the source.

– THE GODDESS

FEBRUARY

M	T	W	T	F	S	S
		1	2	3	4	5
6	7	8	9	10	11	12
13	14	15	16	17	18	19
20	**21**	**22**	**23**	**24**	**25**	**26**
27	28					

MARCH

- What would I like to create, experience and manifest this month?

_____

_____

_____

_____

- What are the important dates for me this month?

_____

_____

- What would give me joy this month?

_____

_____

- What am I devoted to?

_____

_____

- Ideas, musings, actions:

_____

_____

_____

SPRING

THE POWER OF A FRESH START

After a long and cold winter, one of the joys of the new season is to see life encapsulated into new blossoms. I have a peach tree; it's a fairly young one and so not at all big or substantial, and of course it looks pretty straggly in the cold months. And then something magical happens: in early spring, it perks up and forms little nubs on the thin branches and then kaboom – a pink explosion of blossoms!

Just recalling the first sight of these infinitely beautiful and delicate rosy-petalled wonders makes me smile. This fecund act of the plant communicates to us its faith in fruiting and that perhaps we might go along for the same ride.

Spring is a time of growth and momentum, a little promise of more to come. Spring is the time to reach forward towards the future, to watch bud what you may have planned in winter, to trust life a little more. Spring is the time I always take some risks with my work and try new things. Taking what I do in my garden to my life, I'll use this time to grow my seeds of the new, prune back what's in the way and raise my face to the sun, knowing I get a fresh chance at things.

Spring is one of the seasons of transformation that hover between the extremes of winter and summer. This means change is again a major theme of the season, but this time towards growth and extroversion. We too get the chance to throw out what we no longer want or believe, making room for what is new and what may progress us. To resist this is futile.

So, in order to get the most out of the season, we should move, grow, step forward in faith, be fertile in all ways and blossom. This may feel hard after the slower pace of winter, even though, at the end of the day, these actions benefit us and are pleasurable. The two festivals of the Wheel of the Year in spring, Beltane and the spring equinox of Ostara, also centre around these themes.

Spring potion for a fresh start

One of the key symbols and indicators of spring is the blossoming of flowers. I always know its spring where I live from my garden first. I'll observe that many of my trees have tiny buds that begin to swell and the leaves begin to gingerly appear on the formerly ghostly branches and there is an increase in pollinators such as bees.

One of my favourite things to do in spring is to begin to create potions. The growing energy inherent in this season is fantastic for developing potions, especially those made from essential oils or used in baths. Proper potions need to be enlivened. This means you raise power, give that to the potion and tell the potion what to do and what it is for. Also, I often pop potions at this time under a new moon to really layer some 'fresh start' energy.

Here is a recipe I love to create at this time of year. Please note if you are pregnant or have any allergies to any of these plants, do not use it.

You'll need 50 ml of carrier oil such as almond, jojoba or rosehip in a small glass bowl for mixing.

Then add the following high-quality essential oils:
3 drops of bergamot • 3 drops of mandarin • 3 drops of rose geranium or rose otto • 1 drop of lavender or peppermint.

Swirl gently. Hold the bowl in both hands, close your eyes and begin to pull up the energy of the earth and the mother from your feet.

Breathe. On your inhalation, pull up this energy that is your birthright from the feet upwards to your hands and into the bowl.

SAY:

'I hold a bowl of the energy of spring. This is a gift from the goddess, always available to me. I celebrate the season. I celebrate the goddesses of spring who bless us with new beginnings, regeneration, vitality and fresh starts.

'I ask that, when I use this upon myself, I feel this energy through every cell and I am renewed in body, mind and spirit.'

Pour the potion into a dark glass bottle. If you wish, leave it under a new moon for extra oomph.

Massage into your body each morning or when you need a spring lift!

FLORA

GODDESS OF THE MONTH – MARCH

Flora is the ancient Roman goddess of flowers, spring, fertility and youth. Most importantly, she heralds the end of winter and the coming of the warmer months of spring. She is one of the more recognisable goddesses and is always depicted surrounded by and holding plants and blossoms or wearing a flower crown, and she is always young and beautiful.

In the religion of ancient Rome there were 15 important deities who were given their own 'flamen' or priest to signify their stature. There were three 'flamen majores' who would serve the three major gods of Mars, Jupiter and Quintus. The remaining were served by 'flamen minores', and the cult of Flora is one of these.

The Floralis, her official festival, came at the beginning of spring and was a happy and quite wild celebration. Six days long, it included dramas, rituals, the drinking of wine and a hunt. Women were able to dress up in costumes that normally would be banned to them for being too revealing and nakedness was a part of the rituals. Men wore flower crowns, and the sight of an ithyphallic image or a phallus in person was not shocking. It seemed a nice job to be the flamen of Flora!

In her role of heralding spring, all aspects of this including wine growing (important to the Romans), the growth of plants and flowers and the prosperity of the family are focused on and hoped for with her blessing.

Spell for Fertility

To ancient peoples, the idea of fertility wasn't just about whether or not they could conceive a child. They saw the concept of fertility as something much wider and deeper that extended into nature itself. Fertility was what could be grown, produced and created and prosperity in general. In this spell we ask for the help of Flora in extending fertility of all kinds to us.

New moon and any time on the waxing cycle is
the best moon phase for this working.

Gather: a small candle • some resin incense e.g. frankincense, myrrh, benzoin • a glass of wine as an offering • a selection of flowers, as beautiful and as plentiful as you can – *if you can include roses please do, but it's not necessary if you can't; place some in your hair or make a flower crown, and place some on your altar or in a big vase.*

Take a breath. Shut your eyes. Stand up tall. Open a circle if you wish.

Light the candle.

Light the incense and say:

*'Blossoming Flora, ave! I am here to honour your name
and ask you to bless me with fertility.*

'I trust you will be pleased with my offering.'

Pour the wine upon the ground if you are outside or leave it on your altar.

Say:

*'You who herald spring, you who are the embodiment
of growth and fecundity – help me blossom.'*

Tell Flora where you want the blessing of fertility
in your life. Be specific if you can.

Shut your eyes and breathe in the scent of the flowers. Imagine Flora walking towards you bedecked in blossoms and smiling warmly. She places her hands on your shoulders. Everything intensifies – you feel warmth, pleasure, a green energy of fertility flooding your body. Stay there and receive as long as you wish.

Open your eyes, and say:

'Thank you, Flora! I know you have blessed me.'

Blow out the candle with thanks.

WHEEL OF THE YEAR

Ostara

Ah! Here we are at the spring equinox – a time of balance and beauty. At an equinox we have a perfect balance between the elements of light and dark, yet from this time onwards, until Litha, the hours of light will incrementally grow.

Ancient peoples celebrated Ostara because by then the warmth would have settled into the soil in most climates, the harsh grip of winter would be over and real signs of growth would be everywhere. This would be planting time in earnest, when the seeds would be sown at the same time as tending the pregnant farm animals. Plant medicines used over winter would begin to be foraged and restocked.

It would be a busy time too, repairing what was broken during winter storms and removing or resowing into the soil the dead plants. This was building time and villages and farms would again open up and visits and news would be shared. In many ways, this industriousness was a kind of giving back to the earth.

HOW TO CELEBRATE OSTARA

Ostara is a joyous and life-affirming festival. It celebrates steps towards growth and the good things in life.

I prepare my altar with bright spring colours and flowers. I also make sure that I honour the spring goddess Eostre (the Germanic goddess also referred to as Ostara) by placing eggs – both fresh and sculpted – in my decorations. Her myth is a beautiful one; it involves her walking through the countryside on a spring morning bringing warmth back to the land. She finds a tiny bird, almost dead of the cold, and she picks it up and tries to warm it too, but alas it is too far gone. So the goddess transforms it into an egg. The egg hatches and a baby bunny is revealed – a symbol of fertility and love. Hint: now you know where the easter bunny hails from.

Each year, I take a fresh egg and do a special ritual for myself and my garden. I decorate it by writing upon it words and images that represent new intentions and fertile wishes for me and also for my garden. (Remember, fertile can also mean prosperous or growth oriented.) I then go to a place at the time of the equinox and crack the egg, burying it into the earth. I express gratitude for all that is as I'm casting and for all the expansion that I know now will be. I then add some seeds to this area and water it.

27 Monday ◑

Waxing

28 Tuesday ◑

Waxing

1 Wednesday ◑

Waxing

Harvest herbs, fruits and vegetables that grow above the soil at this time.

2 Thursday ◑

Waxing

3 Friday ◑

Waxing

4 Saturday ◑

Waxing

5 Sunday ◑

Waxing

FEBRUARY							MARCH						
M	**T**	**W**	**T**	**F**	**S**	**S**	**M**	**T**	**W**	**T**	**F**	**S**	**S**
			1	2	3	4	5		**1**	**2**	**3**	**4**	**5**
6	7	8	9	10	11	12	6	7	8	9	10	11	12
13	14	15	16	17	18	19	13	14	15	16	17	18	19
20	21	22	23	24	25	26	20	21	22	23	24	25	26
27	**28**						27	28	29	30	31		

6 Monday ☽

Waxing

7 Tuesday ○ Full moon in Virgo 7.40 am EDT

Increase your focus and stamina this full moon. A long-held wish can be granted!

8 Wednesday ☽

Waning

9 Thursday ☽

Waning

10 Friday ◑

Waning

Binding spells are at their most powerful in the waning cycle. What negative behaviour would you like to bind?

11 Saturday ◑

Waning

12 Sunday ◑

Waning

Ride the cycles.

- THE GODDESS

MARCH

M	T	W	T	F	S	S
		1	2	3	4	5
6	**7**	**8**	**9**	**10**	**11**	**12**
13	14	15	16	17	18	19
20	21	22	23	24	25	26
27	28	29	30	31		

13 Monday ◑

Waning

14 Tuesday ◑

Waning

15 Wednesday ◑

Waning

16 Thursday ◑

Waning

Thors-day was named after the Norse god Thor.

17 Friday ◑

Waning

18 Saturday ◑

Waning

19 Sunday ◑

Waning

MARCH

M	T	W	T	F	S	S
		1	2	3	4	5
6	7	8	9	10	11	12
13	**14**	**15**	**16**	**17**	**18**	**19**
20	21	22	23	24	25	26
27	28	29	30	31		

20 Monday ⬤ Ostara, spring equinox 5.24 pm EDT

Dark moon

The hours of night and day are equal, but from tomorrow the days grow longer. The sunshine and warmth are returning to the earth more and more, day by day. Set intentions for health and life balance.

21 Tuesday ☽ New moon in Pisces 1.23 pm EDT

Enjoy this gentle new moon, which is an excellent time for spells for confidence and self-love.

22 Wednesday ◗

Waxing

23 Thursday ◗

Waxing

24 Friday

Waxing

25 Saturday

Waxing

26 Sunday

Waxing

There is someone in the world having their best day ever. There is
someone in the world having their worst day ever. This too shall pass.

– THE GODDESS

MARCH

M	T	W	T	F	S	S
		1	2	3	4	5
6	7	8	9	10	11	12
13	14	15	16	17	18	19
20	**21**	**22**	**23**	**24**	**25**	**26**
27	28	29	30	31		

27 Monday ◑

Waxing

28 Tuesday ◑

Waxing

29 Wednesday ◑

Waxing

30 Thursday ◑

Waxing

31 Friday ☽

Waxing

1 Saturday ☽

Waxing

2 Sunday ☽

Waxing

MARCH							APRIL						
M	**T**	**W**	**T**	**F**	**S**	**S**	**M**	**T**	**W**	**T**	**F**	**S**	**S**
		1	2	3	4	5						1	2
6	7	8	9	10	11	12	3	4	5	6	7	8	9
13	14	15	16	17	18	19	10	11	12	13	14	15	16
20	21	22	23	24	25	26	17	18	19	20	21	22	23
27	**28**	**29**	**30**	**31**			24	25	26	27	28	29	30

APRIL

♦ What would I like to create, experience and manifest this month?

_____

_____

_____

_____

♦ What are the important dates for me this month?

_____

_____

♦ What would give me joy this month?

_____

_____

♦ What am I devoted to?

_____

_____

♦ Ideas, musings, actions:

_____

_____

_____

FREYJA

GODDESS OF THE MONTH — APRIL

Some of the most powerful goddesses in any culture are those who hold the power of both life and death. This duopoly is an interesting one because of the power inherent in both of those aspects. Freyja, the much-loved and -feared goddess of the ancient Norse encapsulates this complexity.

Let's behold her in her powerful form of the battle queen! There she is both beautiful and terrifying on the chaos of a very bloody battlefield, fighting and defending. She holds a bloodied, well-used sword and is naked in all her glory. She cuts down without mercy. Despite the death and destruction around her, she is both intensely inspiring and even desirable to all who fight, as well as absolutely bone-shakingly terrifying to her enemies.

Now balance this: Freyja is also known as the defender of women, a healer and a granter of fertility, and she is a profound patroness of magic and seidr (prophecy). Like many Norse deities, she possesses magical items and talismans including the famous constellation of a necklace called 'Brísingamen' (fire). Wrought from gold and amber, Brísingamen is said to represent the power of the four elements and the fertile power of the synergy of these elements, together. When Freyja dons her necklace, she is irresistible to all!

Freyja was much consulted and prayed to for her wise counsel and for matters of both love and power. Norse women sought her blessings and advice on healing and on magic and sexual matters. Women, in particular, hoped to enter her hall after death (if you had a courageous death – and that included in childbirth or on the battlefield

– Freya may claim you) and many grave rune stones mention that 'this woman went to Freyja'. The runes Fehu and Berkana are most associated with her, although the whole first section (aett) of the Elder Futhark is dedicated to her. Fehu is the rune that represents inner treasures such as power, skill and magic. Berkana represents births and the positive growth of something small to something significant.

SPELL FOR CONFIDENCE WITH RUNE MAGIC

THERE COULD BE NO BETTER GODDESS TO ASSIST US WITH BUILDING OUR OWN PERSONAL POWER, CONFIDENCE AND MAGICAL SKILLS THAN FREYJA. WHEN YOU NEED PHYSICAL OR MENTAL STRENGTH AND THE CONFIDENCE TO TAKE ACTION, SHE CAN ASSIST.

This working needs a representation of the Fehu or Berkana runes. If you don't have a set of runes, simply draw the symbol on a small stone or small piece of wood.

Gather: a small glass of cider or wine • a small candle • the rune of Fehu • something to draw the rune symbol on yourself (*I use an eyeliner pencil because it's easy to wash off when I'm ready*).

LIGHT THE CANDLE AND SAY:

'I call you humbly, great Freyja, battle queen, you who grant life and confidence and work the most powerful of magic. I ask that you assist me today.'

POUR THE OFFERING OF CIDER OR WINE ON THE GROUND. LEAVE A SMALL SIP FOR YOURSELF. SAY:

'Freya, I ask that you bless me with wisdom and magic. I call on you as part of the great tribe of women, for your power and strength.

'Show me how to be powerful! Bless me with your readiness and courage.'

Shut your eyes. Place your awareness in your feet and pull up the energy of the earth. Feel this in every cell. Imagine Freyja standing before you. She holds a sword; she is strong but smiles at you. You are one of her chosen . . . brave, courageous, fertile.

She comes towards you and traces the symbol of Fehu or Berkana on your arm. This is her blessing. You feel every cell in your body respond. You are more confident, powerful, ready. You thank her.

You now open your eyes and draw the symbol on the rune of Fehu on your own skin, on your arm. You are what you have asked to be. Blow out the candle.

Beltane (Bel Tan or Beltaine)

30 APRIL

The wheel has turned and here we are – the most magical night for love and fertility. Wild and full of love magic, Beltane demonstrates the intoxicating energy of life. It is opposite on the Wheel of the Year to Samhain (Hallowe'en), so where Samhain celebrates death and the possibility-filled void, Beltane is the embodiment of lusty life.

Beltane translates as 'good fire', and our ancestors took the returning of the warmth and lifeblood to the land literally by lighting massive torches throughout the country. Feasts and ceremonies accompanied these big bonfires and it was a time of joy and happiness. Some of the earliest Beltane celebrations called for the May Queen and King of the community to be united in ceremony, and then after ritual they would make love upon the earth to bring fertility to the soil. The community would also show their unity on their own land by wildly running, painting symbols upon their bodies, making music, telling stories and feasting.

The modern Beltane is still seen in May Day celebrations where there is dancing around a maypole. The pole is usually wrapped in the colours of red and white and young maidens dance around it. The origins of these dances are fertility based, honouring the forces that bring seeding and growth back to the soil.

Again, like Samhain, the veils between the worlds are at their thinnest, so it is also one of the two best nights of the year to perform divination. Imagine our ancient and not-so-ancient ancestors scrying by the fire, tossing runes or doing ogham wood readings.

HOW TO CELEBRATE BELTANE

As the energy of Beltane is perfect for powerful potion making, it is on this day that I blend and make all kinds of healing salves, salts and potions. I also like to make magical talismans for healing, the attraction of love and prosperity for my clients.

I get up very early on Beltane morning and head for the garden. I light a candle to celebrate the fiery aspect of this festival and I ask for the energetic blessing of this season and that love, fertility and happiness rest upon my house and all in it. I then harvest any herbs and flowers I may need for the day's potion making.

My altar will be decorated with flowers and more flowers! I may do divination. I may also at the end of the day have a lovely blossom-filled bath, perhaps using some of the potions I made earlier. I may decide to do a ritual under the moon in thanks for all I have, and I usually do this sky clad in a reflection of love and trust I have for the way the goddess has made me.

3 Monday ◑

Waxing

4 Tuesday ◑

Waxing

5 Wednesday ◑

Waxing

6 Thursday ○ Full moon in Libra 12.34 am EDT

7 Friday ☽

Waning

8 Saturday ☽

Waning

9 Sunday ☽

Waning

APRIL

M	T	W	T	F	S	S
					1	2
3	**4**	**5**	**6**	**7**	**8**	**9**
10	11	12	13	14	15	16
17	18	19	20	21	22	23
24	25	26	27	28	29	30

10 Monday ☽

Waning

11 Tuesday ☽

Waning

12 Wednesday ☽

Waning

13 Thursday ☽

Waning

14 Friday ☽

Waning

15 Saturday ☽

Waning

16 Sunday ☽

Waning

Under the ground is sacred
Over the ground is holy
Within the sky is reverenced
You'll find me in all.

– THE GODDESS

APRIL

M	T	W	T	F	S	S
					1	2
3	4	5	6	7	8	9
10	**11**	**12**	**13**	**14**	**15**	**16**
17	18	19	20	21	22	23
24	25	26	27	28	29	30

17 Monday ◐

Waning

18 Tuesday ◐

Waning

19 Wednesday ●

Dark moon
Rest and restore.

20 Thursday ☽ New moon in Taurus 12.12 am EDT

A moon to set wishes around improvements to your home or living conditions.

21 Friday

Waxing

22 Saturday

Waxing

23 Sunday

Waxing

APRIL

M	T	W	T	F	S	S
					1	2
3	4	5	6	7	8	9
10	11	12	13	14	15	16
17	**18**	**19**	**20**	**21**	**22**	**23**
24	25	26	27	28	29	30

24 Monday

Waxing

UN World Day for Laboratory Animals. Be conscious about products that have animal testing as part of their manufacture. You can choose cruelty free.

25 Tuesday

Waxing

26 Wednesday

Waxing

27 Thursday

Waxing

28 Friday ☽

Waxing

29 Saturday ☽

Waxing

The veils are thinning as we travel towards Beltane, so why not scry tonight?

30 Sunday ☽

Waxing

Happy Beltane! Celebrate the good (bel) fire (tan). Delight in the most fertile of spring energies and growth today and tonight. Decorate your altar with fresh flowers or make a maypole in your yard.

APRIL

M	T	W	T	F	S	S
					1	2
3	4	5	6	7	8	9
10	11	12	13	14	15	16
17	18	19	20	21	22	23
24	**25**	**26**	**27**	**28**	**29**	**30**

 # MAY

◆ What would I like to create, experience and manifest this month?

_____

_____

_____

_____

◆ What are the important dates for me this month?

_____

_____

◆ What would give me joy this month?

_____

_____

◆ What am I devoted to?

_____

_____

◆ Ideas, musings, actions:

_____

_____

_____

BES

GOD OF THE MONTH – MAY

There is a saying that 'a man's home is his castle'. I believe that everyone deserves to feel safe and secure in their own home and this has always been so. Ancient cultures right across the world also believed this and there have been deities that look after this need specifically.

Bes is the god the Egyptians turned to for the protection of the home and people in it. He and his wife Beset were responsible for the safety and security of the residence. Bes, like many protective gods, is not pretty – after all, a fierce form or countenance is not a hindrance to this set of responsibilities. Unlike many other deities in the pantheon, sculptures and paintings of Bes appeared in almost every home.

Bes is often depicted as a squat figure, all muscles and grimaces, and is usually portrayed in a warrior's tunic to show he is ready for action. He is unusual in the way he is depicted in statues and frescoes, as he is drawn or sculpted front on, not in the usual typical Egyptian style of profile. He is also shown in a looser, more action-oriented stance with an ithyphallic shape (an erect penis). These uncommon depictions show the force of power facing an enemy or bad spirit should they try and challenge him and the sanctity of the home.

Bes is a snake killer, a punisher of thieves, a protector of women and children and an aid to those who are sick or in labour. Bes challenges any evil that might come into the house, and so he was beloved by the people for his good work. Eventually, because of his ability to take away evil and anything that would trouble a household, his influence extended to the positives of music, healing and sexual potency. His cult spread to Phoenicia, Cyprus and even Rome.

HOME PROTECTION SPELL

THIS IS BEST CAST ON A NEW OR FULL MOON.

Gather: a white or gold candle • a gift for Bes – wine or grapes
• some incense *(stick or resin and charcoal)*
• four small crystals – raw quartz is good, but also obsidian.

LIGHT THE CANDLE AND SAY:

*'I call on thee, Bes, mighty protector of my home and family.
I ask you to keep all safe here and evil at bay.'*

Offer the gift to Bes.

LIGHT THE INCENSE AND PASS THE CRYSTALS THROUGH THE SMOKE, SAYING:

'I ask that you, Bes, turn these crystals into talismans of protection. May no evil pass them, may they create a force field in your name, an unbroken line of defence.'

Go and place or bury these crystals in the four points
of the boundary of your property or house.

AS YOU DO THIS, EACH TIME SAY:

'In your name, Bes, I know we are loved and protected.'

Come back to where you started and blow the candle out with thanks.

1 Monday ☽

Waxing

2 Tuesday ☽

Waxing

Tuesday was named after Twia, the Celtic/Germanic god of war and the sky. The Norse god Tyr is also closely identified with this day.

3 Wednesday ☽

Waxing

4 Thursday ☽

Waxing

Sow seeds for plants that are above-ground growers e.g. lettuce, cabbage, mint.

5 Friday ○ Full moon in Scorpio 1.34 pm EDT

A moon to cast for secure boundaries and protection.

Penumbral lunar eclipse visible in New York.

6 Saturday ◑

Waning

7 Sunday ◑

Waning

MAY

M	T	W	T	F	S	S
1	**2**	**3**	**4**	**5**	**6**	**7**
8	9	10	11	12	13	14
15	16	17	18	19	20	21
22	23	24	25	26	27	28
29	30	31				

8 Monday 🌓

Waning

9 Tuesday 🌓

Waning

10 Wednesday 🌓

Waning

11 Thursday 🌓

Waning

12 Friday 🌒

Waning

13 Saturday 🌒

Waning

14 Sunday 🌒

Waning

Rest now
The circle is never ending
Go forth now
The circle in never ending.

– THE GODDESS

MAY

M	T	W	T	F	S	S
1	2	3	4	5	6	7
8	**9**	**10**	**11**	**12**	**13**	**14**
15	16	17	18	19	20	21
22	23	24	25	26	27	28
29	30	31				

15 Monday ◑

Waning

16 Tuesday ◑

Waning

17 Wednesday ◑

Waning

18 Thursday ●

Dark moon

Be still, dream a little, plan yourself a night in.

19 Friday ☽ New moon in Taurus 11.53 am EDT

Set yourself intentions for comfort, ease and what gives you pleasure.

20 Saturday ◐

Waxing

21 Sunday ◐

Waxing

MAY

M	T	W	T	F	S	S
1	2	3	4	5	6	7
8	9	10	11	12	13	14
15	**16**	**17**	**18**	**19**	**20**	**21**
22	23	24	25	26	27	28
29	30	31				

22 Monday ◑

Waxing

23 Tuesday ◑

Waxing

24 Wednesday ◑

Waxing

25 Thursday ◑

Waxing

26 Friday ☽

Waxing

27 Saturday ☽

Waxing

28 Sunday ☽

Waxing

MAY

M	T	W	T	F	S	S
1	2	3	4	5	6	7
8	9	10	11	12	13	14
15	16	17	18	19	20	21
22	**23**	**24**	**25**	**26**	**27**	**28**
29	30	31				

JUNE

- What would I like to create, experience and manifest this month?

_____

_____

_____

_____

- What are the important dates for me this month?

_____

_____

- What would give me joy this month?

_____

_____

- What am I devoted to?

_____

_____

- Ideas, musings, actions:

_____

_____

_____

SUMMER

Vibrating with power!

As long as where you live is not in drought, to walk through a summer garden or landscape is to feel its aliveness. The long, sunny days give plants life and living things energy. There is a buzz around and it's not just the cicadas!

We are at the more open and expansive time of the year and we can feel summer's extroversion. More people are out and about. Social life is outdoors. Our nights are warm enough to sit out under the moon and enjoy. There are more critters exploring the moon time.

While many folks think it's the dark times of winter that are best for magic, I think this is just an old perception linked with the idea that magic is somehow creepy and it has to be hidden or done in the dark. Remembering that real magic is an alchemic activity, weaving different elements together for an intention, summer is as fantastic for casting and magic as winter is, and there is a lot of big energy to capture.

In summer that magical vibe is wonderful for casting for health and vitality, for a happier mood, for less worry and more pleasure. Yes, pleasure! Summer is brilliant for spells to allow more pleasure in your life and to enjoy your life more. Although that may sound strange in a way – that we need to cast for pleasure – I am finding more and more since the last chaotic and difficult few years that there is a lot of anxiety and worry that stops people having a more balanced and enjoyable life.

Summer has always been a sensual time and this can be reflected in our casting. Try going sky clad if you haven't before. Try to include more invocative oils and fragrances in your workings. Try doing more spells outdoors. Try wearing clothes that feel soft and delicious on your skin. Be aware of how the breezes play with your hair, how the sunlight warms your skin and how the music of the birds lifts your spirits. Include all these sense-ual aspects in your casting.

Sparkling mid-summer magic

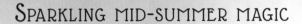

Imagine you were an ancient person excited to be on your way to a big summer solstice festival. Unlike us modern folks, you can't get on a bus or take your own car and drive to this place; you have to prepare to camp and walk the whole way.

So you start your journey on the solstice eve or midsummer's eve. You are on the road with lots of others and there is music, dancing, feasting and drinking at campsites when you rest. It is a joyous and lively time. Yet there are dangers too!

It was said for certain that the Fae were always active along the places that people had to pass through. This was, after all, a time of major magic and the Fae were a particular part of this. The ancients had a healthy respect for the Fae, who to them weren't just pretty sweet 'fairy' figures with gossamer wings. The Fae, if disrespected, could and would 'sweep' you away or take all your possessions. At best, a small mischievous trick could be played on you or an object you need swiped, or at worst you could be 'away with the fairies' and never be seen again!

The travelling folks were always careful to treat the wild lands they passed through with respect and care. You might leave a simple, easy-to-carry offering for them, which would put you in positive stead with the 'good people' and you would get to go on your way safely and you might even get a wish or two granted.

I love midsummer's eve and always mark it in my garden the night before Litha. While I may not be travelling anywhere to see in the solstice, I want to give thanks to the Fae (the spirits of the place) for looking after the garden and to express to them how happy I am that they are there.

My grandmother showed me how to prepare little gifts for this night and I loved doing this when I was small, so if you do have kids, invite them to help. I prepare little plates of food for them, usually some honey from my hive, some cream, strawberries and little sweets or cakes. I make up about three or four, sometimes with a tiny note of thanks to them, and I place each of them where I think they might find them.

These places you will get a feel for and kids are always very good at location finding. Often, they are pretty elbows of tree branches, holes in trunks of trees, mossy rocks, small overhangs where ferns and mushrooms may grow. And here's the strange and beautiful magic: most of the gifts, if not all, will be gone the next day!

TERMINUS

GOD OF THE MONTH – JUNE

In ancient Rome, as you walked around the city, through the suburbs or out further in the countryside, you would often come across a perfectly common thing – a boundary stone. This stone often had a statue of a male god on the top and might offer a name of region or the owner, or a general warning to those who might breach it like *concedo nulli*, meaning 'I yield no ground'.

The god on top of the stone, holding the ground, is Terminus.

Terminus embodies the idea of the sanctity of boundaries. There have always been places where, for cultural or spiritual reasons, certain people were barred. When the idea of ownership became something that could be recorded more accurately, it wasn't just fences or gateways that indicated a boundary but special place stones.

The name 'Terminus' actually means the stone itself.

The Romans specially consecrated these stones with serious ritual. We know this through first-hand accounts recorded by Roman historians of the time. The ritual involved animal sacrifice to Terminus, with the bones and blood of the victim interred with the stone, and the produce of the properties that converged at this spot were also offered to the god. Modern archaeology has dug up the foundations of such boundary stones and there are layers of offerings including seeds, amphoras of wine, jars of honey and bones.

Every year the protection of the boundary stones was renewed. The families of the estates would again come together and do ritual to enliven the boundary stone and ask for the continued protection of Terminus. This too was an opportunity to be neighbourly (or not!) and to discuss the news and work being done on the respective properties.

RITUAL FOR FIRM BOUNDARIES

WHETHER OR NOT YOU NEED THE REINFORCEMENT OF A PROPERTY BOUNDARY OR STRONG PHYSICAL BOUNDARY OR A BEHAVIOURAL BOUNDARY WITH A PERSON, THIS RITUAL CALLING ON TERMINUS CAN ASSIST.

Gather: a candle • a stone as a marker – *if this is for a property, make the stone a decent size (around the size of an average brick); for other needs, you might just use a small stone* • an offering for Terminus – *flowers, honey or candles are perfect.*

You can draw or carve on the stone the Latin words '*concedo nulli*' or '*ire non amplius*' (meaning 'go no further') and a thank you to Terminus in any way you might wish.

Do this spell ideally in the daytime at dawn or at midday. If you are doing a spell to strengthen the boundaries of a property, stand where you will place the stone. Any other kind of boundary can be within your home if you wish.

LIGHT A CANDLE AND SAY:

'Ave, Terminus! I humbly ask for your strength in creating a sacred boundary for my property/myself,'

AND EXPLAIN WHERE YOU WANT THE BOUNDARY AND WHY.

'Please grace me with your protection and allow those whose intention is to tread or transgress over this boundary to go no further.'

PLACE THE STONE AND SAY:

'I place this marker in your name.'

If you are performing this for a behavioural boundary, hold the stone in your hand or pocket and keep it with you.

Blow out the candle and give thanks to Terminus.

WHEEL OF THE YEAR

Litha

SUMMER SOLSTICE, 21 JUNE 10.57 AM EDT

If you are someone who loves to draw up energy from the earth and so is sensitive to the different feels and textures of this at different times of the year, you know how Litha energy is. It is big. It is full. It is fast. It is expansive. And it's worth waiting for!

Litha is a solstice festival – in fact, the most powerful one in each year. We get to experience the longest day of the year and the shortest night. This peak solar experience was a very big deal for many cultures across the world, not for the least reason that it was a key marker for growth in the year. After this time, the daylight hours slowly grow shorter and the night hours grow longer. It is a time to understand that the cycle is always in action and that the colder and darker times will indeed return eventually.

Litha therefore was and is a celebration of 'now' – right now, the heat is here, everything is at its energetic peak and there seems no limit to our confidence, growth and expansion. It is big magic!

HOW TO CELEBRATE LITHA

The full and powerful vitality of Litha allows us to concentrate on two main areas for our spell work should we choose to do this. The first area is that of prosperity. Litha has always been a wonderful time to work on our wealth and prosperity as well as our generosity. I always make talismans of prosperity just before Litha and leave them out under the solar energies to charge up.

The second area is that of health. Litha as I mentioned is big sun-driven energy, and this lends itself to burning away our imbalances and inviting in vitality and good health. If you wish to make adjustments and changes to the way you think of or treat your body, Litha is a fantastic time to start.

Litha being a solar festival is also linked with the masculine energies. It's a chance to honour the masculine Divine in your life and the masculine aspects of yourself. I ensure I make offerings or devotions to all the wonderful gods I work with in thanks for their support.

A Litha altar is a bright and sunny one! It is prepared a few days prior and it will feature flame colours, gold, coins and often bright flowers like calendula or sunflowers.

The sun rises early on Litha so I get up just before sunrise so I can catch every minute of this long light-filled day. I make it a priority as the sun rises over the horizon to take the time to pull up energy from the earth and allow it to fill my body with energy. Litha is also the ultimate time to make aqua sol (sun water) because of the long daylight hours on this day.

29 Monday ◑

Waxing

30 Tuesday ◑

Waxing

31 Wednesday ◑

Waxing

1 Thursday ◑

Waxing

2 Friday ◐

Waxing

3 Saturday ◯ Full moon in Sagittarius 11.41 pm EDT

Cast spells with the intention to improve communication and friendships of all kinds.

4 Sunday ◑

Waning

MAY							JUNE						
M	T	W	T	F	S	S	M	T	W	T	F	S	S
1	2	3	4	5	6	7				**1**	**2**	**3**	**4**
8	9	10	11	12	13	14	5	6	7	8	9	10	11
15	16	17	18	19	20	21	12	13	14	15	16	17	18
22	23	24	25	26	27	28	19	20	21	22	23	24	25
29	**30**	**31**					26	27	28	29	30		

5 Monday ◑

Waning

6 Tuesday ◑

Waning

7 Wednesday ◑

Waning

8 Thursday ◑

Waning

9 Friday ☽

Waning

10 Saturday ☽

Waning

11 Sunday ☽

Waning

The wheel always turns.

- THE GODDESS

M	T	W	T	F	S	S
			1	2	3	4
5	**6**	**7**	**8**	**9**	**10**	**11**
12	13	14	15	16	17	18
19	20	21	22	23	24	25
26	27	28	29	30		

12 Monday ◐

Waning

13 Tuesday ◐

Waning

14 Wednesday ◐

Waning

15 Thursday ◐

Waning

You might like to prepare your wishes and celebrations for Litha coming next week!

16 Friday ◐

Waning

17 Saturday ●

Dark moon

Is there a habit or pattern you'd like to shake off? Cast to rid yourself of them tonight.

18 Sunday ☽ New moon in Cancer 12.37 am EDT

Give yourself a break and know that you too are worthy of a fresh start. A beautiful moon for the building of healthy self-esteem and body image.

We do not have to be all things to all people.

- THE GODDESS

JUNE						
M	T	W	T	F	S	S
			1	2	3	4
5	6	7	8	9	10	11
12	13	14	15	16	17	18
19	20	21	22	23	24	25
26	27	28	29	30		

19 Monday ◑

Waxing

20 Tuesday ◑

Waxing

Mid-summer's eve: get your sparkle on because this is certainly one of the most magical nights of the whole year. We honour the Fae in our gardens and wild places this evening, so start your preparations early. This is a wonderful festival to involve your kids, because who doesn't love a fairy. Traditional gifts of strawberries, honey and milk plus pretty objects are left out in the wild places for the local Fae. Give thanks to them for the protective work they do in your neck of the woods!

21 Wednesday ◑ Litha – summer solstice 10.57 am EDT

Waxing

This is a day of BIG power so I suggest you rise early, light a candle and catch as much energy as you can. This is the day to honour the masculine Divine in all its forms and celebrate the year's biggest festival of the sun. A perfect time to cast spells for health and wealth.

22 Thursday ◑

Waxing

23 Friday ◑

Waxing

24 Saturday ◑

Waxing

25 Sunday ◑

Waxing

Allow all the elements to work within you.
The drive of fire, the flow of water
The intellect of air, the loving groundedness of earth.
All these are yours.

– THE GODDESS

M	T	W	T	F	S	S
			1	2	3	4
5	6	7	8	9	10	11
12	13	14	15	16	17	18
19	**20**	**21**	**22**	**23**	**24**	**25**
26	27	28	29	30		

26 Monday ◑

Waxing

A good day to trim your hair if you want it to grow.

27 Tuesday ◑

Waxing

28 Wednesday ◑

Waxing

29 Thursday ◑

Waxing

30 Friday ☽

Waxing

End of the financial year. Consider how you would like to improve your finances for next year.

1 Saturday ☽

Waxing

Saturday was named after the Roman god Saturn.

2 Sunday ☽

Waxing

Dream AND do.

- THE GODDESS

JUNE								JULY						
M	T	W	T	F	S	S		M	T	W	T	F	S	S
			1	2	3	4							1	2
5	6	7	8	9	10	11		3	4	5	6	7	8	9
12	13	14	15	16	17	18		10	11	12	13	14	15	16
19	20	21	22	23	24	25		17	18	19	20	21	22	23
26	**27**	**28**	**29**	**30**				24	25	26	27	28	29	30
								31						

JULY

- ◆ What would I like to create, experience and manifest this month?

_____

_____

_____

_____

- ◆ What are the important dates for me this month?

_____

_____

- ◆ What would give me joy this month?

_____

_____

- ◆ What am I devoted to?

_____

_____

- ◆ Ideas, musings, actions:

_____

_____

_____

FORSETI

GOD OF THE MONTH – JULY

In the mythos of the Norse, there was a god who kept a hall and court that was a haven of peace. It was so because of his wisdom and energy towards good counsel, justice and reconciliation.

This place was called Glitnir (shining) and it was beautifully constructed of pillars of golden light, with silver ceilings, and like a lighthouse could be seen for miles. Particularly in the darkest times – whether this was the deepest winter or the harshest wars – Glitnir shone like a beacon for all.

The owner of such a place and the key to its calm and fame was Forseti. The son of the beautiful and good god Baldr and his wife Nanna, a goddess of peace and the moon, it is no wonder their son was such a luminous example.

It was said that if there were any who walked into his hall who were fighting and angry, there would be negotiations of such high quality that often the two would not just be satisfied but reconciled. If there had been a misjustice, Forseti was the one to repair this or expose it clearly for all to see.

All of us, at some time in our lives, need the calm of good counsel and fair negotiation. We also may need justice to be fairly done or simply that a light shine for us to see examples of goodness and virtue. Maybe we need help to reconcile with someone.

Perhaps we need Forseti more than ever.

Ritual for justice and wise counsel

I PREFER TO CAST THIS SPELL ON A NEW MOON OR WAXING
CYCLE, BUT ANY TIME YOU NEED IT IS THE BEST TIME.

Gather: three silver or gold candles – *tealights are fine*
• a glass of wine, honey mead or cider.

LIGHT THE FIRST CANDLE AND SAY:

'I ask for your wise counsel, Forseti of Glitnir. I ask you to turn your eyes upon me.'

LIGHT THE SECOND CANDLE AND SAY:

*'Son of Nanna and Baldr, shining one, I light the flame in your
name. I ask that fairness and light come to my situation.'*

THEN EXPLAIN THE SITUATION. LIGHT THE THIRD CANDLE AND SAY:

*'Forseti, you who bring calm and peace to unreconciled
situations, take me away from the chaos of others.'*

Close your eyes and imagine you are in the shining golden hall of
light with the wise Forseti. Feel his blessing, his calm, the certainty
that all will come to justice. Stay there as long as you wish.

WHEN YOU ARE READY, OPEN YOUR EYES AND HOLD UP
THE GLASS OF WINE, CIDER OR MEAD AND SAY:

*'I ask for your blessing and assistance. I trust all will be
well and I will act in your guidance. Skol!'*

Pour the wine on the ground or leave it on your altar –
all except for a sip you'll share with the god.

Blow out each candle with thanks.

3 Monday ○ Full moon in Capricorn 7.38 am EDT

The time to plan is here. Cast for BIG things.

4 Tuesday ◑

Waning

5 Wednesday ◑

Waning

6 Thursday ◑

Waning

7 Friday 🌗

Waning

8 Saturday 🌗

Waning

9 Sunday 🌗

Waning

Can you feel it?
The divine change that is upon you?

– THE GODDESS

JULY

M	T	W	T	F	S	S
					1	2
3	**4**	**5**	**6**	**7**	**8**	**9**
10	11	12	13	14	15	16
17	18	19	20	21	22	23
24	25	26	27	28	29	30
31						

10 Monday ◑

Waning

11 Tuesday ◑

Waning

12 Wednesday ◑

Waning

13 Thursday ◑

Waning

14 Friday ☽

Waning

15 Saturday ☽

Waning

16 Sunday ●

Dark moon

Restore yourself. Perhaps sit outside and watch the shining stars or have a fragrant bath.

Dance within the circle
We are all within it
Winged, scaled, furred
And you.

– THE GODDESS

M	T	W	T	F	S	S
					1	2
3	4	5	6	7	8	9
10	11	12	13	14	15	16
17	18	19	20	21	22	23
24	25	26	27	28	29	30
31						

17 Monday ☽ New moon in Cancer 2.31 pm EDT

Take a deep breath and understand that you can choose how you respond to life – rather than react to it.

18 Tuesday ◑

Waxing

19 Wednesday ◑

Waxing

20 Thursday ◑

Waxing

21 Friday ☽

Waxing

22 Saturday ☽

Waxing

23 Sunday ☽

Waxing

(((((radiate calm)))))

- THE GODDESS

JULY

M	T	W	T	F	S	S
					1	2
3	4	5	6	7	8	9
10	11	12	13	14	15	16
17	**18**	**19**	**20**	**21**	**22**	**23**
24	25	26	27	28	29	30
31						

24 Monday

Waxing

25 Tuesday

Waxing

Harvest above-ground vegetables this week.

26 Wednesday

Waxing

27 Thursday

Waxing

28 Friday ☽

Waxing

29 Saturday ☽

Waxing

30 Sunday ☽

Waxing

The cycle flows forward
Light returns.

– THE GODDESS

JULY

M	T	W	T	F	S	S
					1	2
3	4	5	6	7	8	9
10	11	12	13	14	15	16
17	18	19	20	21	22	23
24	**25**	**26**	**27**	**28**	**29**	**30**
31						

AUGUST

- What would I like to create, experience and manifest this month?

_____

_____

_____

_____

- What are the important dates for me this month?

_____

_____

- What would give me joy this month?

_____

_____

- What am I devoted to?

_____

_____

- Ideas, musings, actions:

_____

_____

_____

IRIS

GODDESS OF THE MONTH – AUGUST

Sometimes you just need something beautiful to look at to feel better. We know that being in the beauty of nature can lower our blood pressure, stress levels, boost happy hormones like dopamine and give us a feeling of well-being and gratitude. Of course, what constitutes beauty is subjective; however, there are certain universals like sunrises, sunsets and expansive vistas, and certainly rainbows would be included.

The rainbow has been a source of human happiness and wonder since we became human. While we know now scientifically why rainbows are formed the way they are and why they are so colourful, our ancient ancestors saw them often as messages or messengers from, or a link to, the gods. Our beautiful goddess of the month is Iris, the Greek goddess of the rainbow.

The word 'Iris' literally means 'rainbow' in Greek. The daughter of Thaumas, a sea god, and the sea nymph Electra, Iris was an important messenger of the gods and featured in many myths. She was often pictured as a golden-winged woman and, like Hermes, she carried a caduceus.

It was Iris that Zeus sent to Demeter to try and persuade her to bring back all life to the earth and alleviate famine, after the kidnap of her daughter Persephone. It was Iris who told Menelaus of his wife Helen's secret in sailing to Troy. Perhaps the most famous myth about Iris is when she carried a pottery jar full of the waters of the deathly River Styx to induce sleep in those who may perjure themselves.

Iris also was worshipped by the Greeks for her help in assisting their prayers and wishes in reaching the gods and for granting wishes herself. It is thought that the wishing upon rainbows superstition started with Iris and her worship, and the ancient Greeks, upon seeing a rainbow, would see this as a good and happy omen that brought opportunity.

Spell for happiness and gratitude

THIS IS A BEAUTIFUL SPELL YOU CAN CAST ON ANY PART OF THE MOON CYCLE, AND OF COURSE IT'S FUN TO DO WITH YOUR KIDS TOO.

Ahead of time, think about a few things that make you happy. Think also about the last time you saw a rainbow and try and recall this in your mind clearly.

Make some aqua luna (water left out under a full moon) for use in this spell.

On your altar or where you are casting, make up a 'cornucopia' – a selection of seasonal foods and herbs. Make this as attractive as you can.

The best time to cast is during a new moon to full moon.

Gather: a candle • an A3 piece of paper • crayons, pencils or paints the colours of the rainbow.

LIGHT THE CANDLE AND SAY:

'I call thee, Iris, goddess of the rainbows, messenger of the gods! You who are swift footed and bright and beautiful, assist me in my intentions.

'I come before you today to ask you for your blessings of happiness upon me.'

Draw a rainbow on the blank page. As you do so, think about the last time you saw an actual rainbow and how good it made you feel. Be mindful as you draw only of this. When you are finished, shut your eyes. Allow that feeling of happiness and wonder to spread through every cell. Flood your body with goodwill and gratitude.

WHEN YOU ARE READY, OPEN YOUR EYES AND SAY:

'I ask that I remember the wonder of this moment and the joy of the rainbow. I take in this beauty and your blessings, Iris!'

CLAP THREE TIMES AND SAY:

'It is as I have asked.'

Thank Iris. Blow out the candle. Tape the drawing to a window or a wall to remind you to be grateful.

WHEEL OF THE YEAR

Lammas

1 August

Lammas is the first of the harvest festivals for the year. If you looked back on the agricultural lives of people across Europe a few thousand years ago, you'd see villages and collectives working diligently towards the bounty of harvest. No supermarkets back then – what was grown or hunted was for survival.

Villagers would gather together to assist with the harvest itself often, with groups harvesting one field or area and then another owned by someone else. This communal effort not only helped get the job done faster and perhaps allowed for some trading to be engaged in, but it was a great way for folks to come together and see each other. News was swapped, stories told and more than one match made!

I love the harvest festivals because they give me an excuse to feel grateful in a real way. Although I have a practice that often touches on gratitude, actually having a proper festival that deeply engages with it is useful. It allows us to really examine and look back at what is working or has worked for us and what hasn't (and we learned from), and actually seeing how far we have progressed is something inherently valuable.

HOW TO CELEBRATE LAMMAS

The place that most people start celebrating Lammas is in their kitchen! Baking bread is an early tradition of harvest festivals like Lammas. I am no great cook, but even I will start the day off by baking a loaf or attempting some biscuits or cakes. I normally try and prepare the dough and let it rise the night before and then bake it on Lammas morning.

Lammas altars often feature foods of the season. I think about what represents the harvest where I am and then I find a couple of small baskets and fill them with fruits and whatever I have in my garden growing at that time. The Lammas altar colours are gold, orange, brown and dark green to represent the shades of agriculture.

As all of the Wheel of the Year festivals are generally to be celebrated with friends, having people over for a feast is a joyful way to involve others. As this is a festival of harvest, everyone brings something to contribute – from candles to their favourite dish, fruit from their trees or something they have made to decorate the table.

When the feasting is done, we create a circle and light candles and share with each other what we are grateful for right now. We discuss too what we have achieved thus far – a kind of personal harvest, if you like. I always feel that it's a life-affirming thing to do this in front of and with my friends. Being able to celebrate and mark each other's triumphs is a positive and loving thing to do.

31 Monday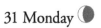

Waxing

1 Tuesday ◯ Full moon in Aquarius 2.31 pm EDT

Super full moon

A big moon that inspires you to do things differently and to take a chance! Cast for innovations and the success of new projects.

Lammas – the traditional time of first harvest and a time of gratitude. Look upon the harvest of your life thus far, mark it and express your gratitude.

2 Wednesday ◗

Waning

3 Thursday ◗

Waning

4 Friday ◑

Waning

5 Saturday ◑

Waning

6 Sunday ◑

Waning

JULY							AUGUST						
M	T	W	T	F	S	S	M	T	W	T	F	S	S
					1	2	**1**	**2**	**3**	**4**	**5**	**6**
3	4	5	6	7	8	9	7	8	9	10	11	12	13
10	11	12	13	14	15	16	14	15	16	17	18	19	20
17	18	19	20	21	22	23	21	22	23	24	25	26	27
24	25	26	27	28	29	30	28	29	30	31			
31													

7 Monday ☽

Waning

8 Tuesday ☽

Waning

9 Wednesday ☽

Waning

10 Thursday ☽

Waning

11 Friday ☽

Waning

12 Saturday ☽

Waning

13 Sunday ☽

Waning

Pull up what you need from the earth.
You will never be alone,
I await you.

– THE GODDESS

AUGUST

M	T	W	T	F	S	S
	1	2	3	4	5	6
7	**8**	**9**	**10**	**11**	**12**	**13**
14	15	16	17	18	19	20
21	22	23	24	25	26	27
28	29	30	31			

14 Monday ◗

Waning

15 Tuesday ●

Dark moon

Joyfully: Let. It. Go.

16 Wednesday ☽ New moon in Leo 5.38 am EDT

Micro new moon

A night to cast for personal power and confidence.

17 Thursday ◖

Waxing

18 Friday ◑

Waxing

19 Saturday ◑

Waxing

20 Sunday ◑

Waxing

Can you feel the flowers in your blood,
For it is spring.

- THE GODDESS

AUGUST

M	T	W	T	F	S	S
		1	2	3	4	5	6
7	8	9	10	11	12	13
14	**15**	**16**	**17**	**18**	**19**	**20**
21	22	23	24	25	26	27
28	29	30	31			

21 Monday ◑

Waxing

22 Tuesday ◑

Waxing

23 Wednesday ◑

Waxing

24 Thursday ◑

Waxing

25 Friday

Waxing

26 Saturday

Waxing

27 Sunday

Waxing

A U G U S T

AUGUST

M	T	W	T	F	S	S
		1	2	3	4	5	6
7	8	9	10	11	12	13
14	15	16	17	18	19	20
21	**22**	**23**	**24**	**25**	**26**	**27**
28	29	30	31			

SEPTEMBER

◆ What would I like to create, experience and manifest this month?

_____

_____

_____

_____

◆ What are the important dates for me this month?

_____

_____

◆ What would give me joy this month?

_____

_____

◆ What am I devoted to?

_____

_____

◆ Ideas, musings, actions:

_____

_____

_____

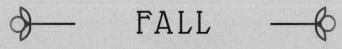

FALL

The cycle transforms

The first sign that things are changing from the big heat of summer is, for me, always felt in my body. It's not just that the temperature changes and we start to get cool mornings and nights; it's that my body begins to feel a bit more constructed and rigid. Perhaps I'm a bit sore in the mornings or that languid looseness in my limbs during extroverted summer begins to fade. So, in answer to this change, I change. I do more yoga to help that body change, I eat differently and I throw on another layer to keep those bones warm.

It is in these transitional seasons – fall and spring – that we most feel the transformational turn of the seasonal wheel. We get to slowly move away from the extreme seasons and experience something new, but since we have been at the extremes for some time that feeling and adaptation may be hard to kick. We are creatures of habit!

It is a season during which I love to observe the reality of change. We see some plants change their colours and some completely die back. We of course see the colours of the fall foliage. We feel the winds change direction, and we get new birds visiting and some leaving for warmer climes. The energy is slowing, preparing us for winter.

To me, the joy of this season is to ride this change and not resist it. While many of us love the warmth and extroversion of summer, the wheel turns, as always, and we find ourselves on a different rhythm.

CLEARING SPELL FOR FALL

EVERYONE KNOWS ABOUT 'SPRING CLEANING' BUT THE TRANSITIONAL
SEASON OF FALL NEEDS ITS OWN CLEARING. SOMETIMES EVERY HOME
OR OFFICE NEEDS A POSITIVE CHANGE OF ENERGY AND A SPACE
CLEARING. HERE IS A SIMPLE AND SEASONAL WAY TO DO THIS.

Gather: a fall leaf that is changing or has changed colour *(one per person
casting)* • a permanent marker • a candle • frankincense resin and charcoal,
or if this is too hard to get, any incense will do • a flameproof bowl or cauldron.

Do this spell on a waning cycle or on a dark moon.
Ahead of time, write down on the leaf with the permanent
marker one thing that you would like cleared or changed.

LIGHT THE CANDLE.

LIGHT THE FRANKINCENSE RESIN AND CHARCOAL.

SAY OUT LOUD:

*'I humbly speak to all the energies of the changing earth.
The wind, the weather, the longer nights and the shorter days. I trust that
what I/we wish to change will change. That it will transform for our good.'*

Hold up your leaf. Speak about the change that you want. If you are with
others, each person should preferably state out loud what it represents and where
they want change but they can do this privately in their mind if they wish.

After each person holds up their leaf and expresses this, everyone should
say, *'Yes! May this be so!'* And the person should then set the leaf on fire
from the candle and carefully place it in the bowl or cauldron.

Once everyone has burnt all their leaves, thank all the energies that
have assisted you and each other for the support you will extend.

Express one step you'll take towards your intention.

Blow out the candle.

NANTOSUELTA

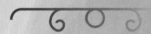

There are thousands of faces of the goddess. Sometimes the name of a goddess fades into the folds of history due to invasion, war, even systems like the patriarchy, and she transforms and morphs into a different form or name. I think it's important that we keep the name of ancient goddesses alive in their earlier forms if we can because not only does this have spiritual value, but sometimes the attributes of the deity are well worth working with and honouring.

Allow me to introduce you to Nantosuelta just in case you aren't aware of her. She is a goddess of the Celts and evidence of her worship has been found as far as the Alsace region bordering France and Germany. Nantosuelta is a goddess of duopoly – she is both fire and water, solar and lunar, at war and at peace. It is believed that her form and attributes began to be incorporated into that of the Morrigan and the black crow birds that are part of symbology attest to this.

Nantosuelta is importantly a goddess who rules nature, both wild and that of agriculture. She is normally pictured with a round house around her, which links her to the idea of spirits of the local places, and in this we see an obvious link to the Fae. Her name comes from the root words for 'winding stream' and 'sun in the valley'.

She is also a healer of the 'nature' of humans and provides, through her protection and sovereignty over the land, everything that humans need to survive.

She is a healer of the body and a giver of growth and vitality. At the same time, in her crow form, she flies over a battlefield to quickly assess the situation and strike at her enemies.

In ancient ceremonies, she was often invoked to secure and bond alliances, and it was said she would punish breaches of vows with death.

Invocation to Nantosuelta for health

THE DAYTIME HOURS OF THE DAY OF THE FULL MOON IS A GREAT TIME TO CAST THIS SPELL. NANTOSUELTA HAS BOTH A SOLAR AND LUNAR ASSOCIATION. YOU WILL BE MAKING AQUA SOL (BLESSED SUN WATER) AS PART OF THIS WORKING.

Gather: a large open bowl full of water • a water bottle to store your water for later • a yellow or gold candle • a small handful of grain *(wheat, oats, rice for example).*

Place your bowl full of water out in the sun at the hottest part of the day, which is usually between midday and 2 pm.

AS YOU PLACE THIS SAY:

'I ask you goddess Nantosuelta to bless this water. I hereby make aqua sol.'

Once you have left the water out for at least an hour, pour it into a water bottle.

LIGHT THE CANDLE AND SAY:

'You who are of both fire and water, of sun and of moon and rule all of wild nature, Nantosuelta, I call you!'

TAKE THE GRAIN IN YOUR HAND AND THROW IT GENTLY UPON THE EARTH AND SAY:

'I offer you the grains of the earth.'

HOLD THE WATER BOTTLE IN YOUR HAND AND SAY:

'I would ask that you bless me with robust health and sparkling vitality. I ask that you lend me your energy of both the motivation of fire and flowfulness of water and that you heal any imbalances within me. I ask this, knowing all will be as I have asked if it be for my highest good.'

Take some sips of the aqua sol. Allow the blessing to infuse every cell.

Thank Nantosuelta and blow out the candle.

WHEEL OF THE YEAR

Mabon

Mabon is the first equinox of the year. An equinox is when the hours of light and dark are equal. This balance happens twice a year and is recognised as a sacred time for many cultures throughout history.

Mabon is the last (or second) harvest festival and of course this was important to mark for those folks who worked on the land. These markers were important because the weather and the cycles dictated what to plant, and when to plant and harvest. They knew that from the day after an equinox the daylight hours would change. In this case, until the next equinox, daylight would reduce a little each day and so the weather would cool. Winter was on the horizon, so Mabon signalled the time to harvest and prepare for the leaner times coming.

Seeds were stored, food preserved, fruits made into jams and pastes. The last of the honey was collected from the hives and the health of the bees was checked before winter. Plants and meats were dried. Herbs were collected for medicines. Organised hunts were stepped up in frequency. Shelters were repaired and made strong to stand against the powers of blizzards and harsh, cold storms. Again, we see the community coming together to do these things and the collective becoming important.

HOW TO CELEBRATE MABON

There is a distinct magic about the times of balance. A shimmering kind of magic where we get the opportunity – just for a time – to hover in between worlds and elements. Equinoxes are such times. They remind us that it is necessary to find moderation and balance for our mind, body and spirit. Any habits that are leaning towards the extreme we can look at transforming.

I also, quite traditionally, use this time to collect herbs that have reached their zenith and dry them for my magical and medicinal use. I also make sure I've been collecting the seeds of those plants in my garden that have reached that stage. I keep some of these for spring planting but I also love to give these as gifts or swap them with my friends who love to grow and garden too.

I make jam, chutneys and pickles, which preserve the fruits and vegetables of the season and are always a delight to open in the depths of late winter. Yes, of course you can buy commercial brands of all these things pretty much all year round these days, but to actually open a jar of jam that you have created from your own harvested fruit, in a season where this fruit is just a dream now, is to me a kind of magic!

28 Monday ◑

Waxing

29 Tuesday ◑

Waxing

30 Wednesday ○ Full moon in Pisces 9.35 pm EDT

Super full moon

Blue moon

Delight in a moon that brings harmony and understanding. It's a blue moon too, so ask for a long-held wish to be manifested.

A wonderful night for making aqua luna (moon water). Leave the purest water you can find in a white or silver bowl under the moon and retrieve and bottle prior to dawn. Use this in your potions, space clearing and even your bath!

31 Thursday

Waning

1 Friday ☽

Waning

2 Saturday ☽

Waning

3 Sunday ☽

Waning

AUGUST							SEPTEMBER						
M	T	W	T	F	S	S	M	T	W	T	F	S	S
	1	2	3	4	5	6					1	2	3
7	8	9	10	11	12	13	4	5	6	7	8	9	10
14	15	16	17	18	19	20	11	12	13	14	15	16	17
21	22	23	24	25	26	27	18	19	20	21	22	23	24
28	29	30	31				25	26	27	28	29	30	

4 Monday ◑

Waning

5 Tuesday ◑

Waning

6 Wednesday ◑

Waning

7 Thursday ◑

Waning

8 Friday ☽

Waning

9 Saturday ☽

Waning

10 Sunday ☽

Waning

Shining brightly
Made of stars
. . . You.

– THE GODDESS

SEPTEMBER						
M	T	W	T	F	S	S
				1	2	3
4	5	6	7	8	9	10
11	12	13	14	15	16	17
18	19	20	21	22	23	24
25	26	27	28	29	30	

11 Monday ◐

Waning

12 Tuesday ◐

Waning

13 Wednesday ⚫

Dark moon

Let go of old ideas of perfection and self-doubt.

14 Thursday ☽ New moon in Virgo 9.39 pm EDT

Ideal for casting spells for justice and to clear pathways from old trauma. This is a moon to help consolidate a clean, clear new strategy.

15 Friday ◑

Waxing

16 Saturday ◑

Waxing

17 Sunday ◑

Waxing

SEPTEMBER

M	T	W	T	F	S	S
				1	2	3
4	5	6	7	8	9	10
11	**12**	**13**	**14**	**15**	**16**	**17**
18	19	20	21	22	23	24
25	26	27	28	29	30	

18 Monday ☽

Waxing

19 Tuesday ☽

Waxing

20 Wednesday ☽

Waxing

21 Thursday ☽

Waxing

22 Friday ☽

Waxing

23 Saturday ☽ Mabon, fall equinox 2.50 am EDT

Waxing

A night to release your regrets!

The second harvest festival of the year. Recognise the harvest of your life! Be grateful for what you have. Take stock of what has served you and what has not. Let go of what you no longer need and decide to transform for the better.

24 Sunday ☽

Waxing

Sometimes
We cease to see the magic within us
And yet it is there.
Allow

– THE GODDESS

SEPTEMBER						
M	T	W	T	F	S	S
				1	2	3
4	5	6	7	8	9	10
11	12	13	14	15	16	17
18	19	20	21	22	23	24
25	26	27	28	29	30	

25 Monday ◐

Waxing

26 Tuesday ◐

Waxing

27 Wednesday ◐

Waxing

28 Thursday ◐

Waxing

29 Friday ◯ Full moon in Aries 5.57 am EDT

A night of power to set new goals and intentions. It is also a great night to do binding spells. Mind your ethics, though!

30 Saturday ◑

Waning

1 Sunday ◑

Waning

SEPTEMBER							OCTOBER						
M	T	W	T	F	S	S	M	T	W	T	F	S	S
				1	2	3							1
4	5	6	7	8	9	10	2	3	4	5	6	7	8
11	12	13	14	15	16	17	9	10	11	12	13	14	15
18	19	20	21	22	23	24	16	17	18	19	20	21	22
25	**26**	**27**	**28**	**29**	**30**		23	24	25	26	27	28	29
							30	31					

OCTOBER

- ◆ What would I like to create, experience and manifest this month?

_____

_____

_____

_____

- ◆ What are the important dates for me this month?

_____

_____

- ◆ What would give me joy this month?

_____

_____

- ◆ What am I devoted to?

_____

_____

- ◆ Ideas, musings, actions:

_____

_____

_____

TAMAR

GODDESS OF THE MONTH – OCTOBER

In the mythos of the country Georgia, before the coming of Christianity, there was a great goddess spoken of named Tamar.

Tamar loves the land she has as her realm and lives in a palace in the high mountains. She rules over the plants and all growing things. It is she whom prayers are sent to for good bountiful harvests and healthy animals. She loves the fruits borne by the trees, the seeds of plants, all the animals and particularly birds.

It is understood that birds, the nightingales and storks, had built her palace and for such a magical home she is so grateful. She wishes that the land would be fruitful all the year and that the snows would never come and the birds didn't have to go away.

And so she decides to capture the Morning Star and Master of Winter, Dilis Varskulavi. She thinks if she can capture and hold him, he cannot work his magic and create snows and bring the bitter cold to the land.

So she rides out on her fierce serpent, her dark hair flying behind her and her hands upon the gold reigns and bridle of her mount. She bravely captures Morning Star and holds him captive for as long as she can. She is successful for many months and controls all the weather.

However, he eventually breaks free of her after a time, since he too is as strong and powerful as she is, and his breath begins to bring ice and snow. Until Tamar can

can recapture Dilis, winter will have its hold upon the earth. This is a story of the power of cycles and of how we are more benefited by riding them than resisting them.

And here, now, we find ourselves riding the same cycles towards winter. We begin to enjoy the last harvests of our gardens and the next month or so we enjoy the warmer weather, but we know that winter is coming.

SPELL FOR A BRAVE AND BOUNTIFUL LIFE

AHEAD OF TIME, CONSIDER SPECIFICALLY WHERE YOU WANT MORE BOUNTY AND/OR BRAVERY. IS IT A BETTER JOB, A HEALTHIER BODY, MORE PROSPERITY, A MORE FECUND GARDEN?

This spell is best done on the waxing part of the moon cycle.
If this can be done outdoors, please do.

Gather: a white, orange or gold candle • a feather or piece of snake skin as an offering to Tamar • some seeds.

LIGHT THE CANDLE AND SAY:

'Tamar, brave goddess of a rich bountiful life. I call your name in the humble hope that you will assist me please.'

HOLD UP THE FEATHER OR SNAKE SKIN AND SAY:

'I offer this gift to you, brave and powerful Tamar!'

Place this on the ground in the garden or on your altar.

Tell Tamar where you would like to increase your bounty or your bravery.

EXPLAIN ALL THIS TO HER OUT LOUD AND THEN COMPLETE THIS WITH:

'You who control the weather, you who bring to fruition all things, I humbly ask for your support.'

Now take the seeds in your hands. Close your eyes and imagine them growing into their maturity, full richness and bounty.

OPEN YOUR EYES AND SAY:

'I plant these in your honour Tamar!'

(Later, plant the seeds and look after them.)

As always for your participation, take one action, no matter how small, toward your intention.

WHEEL OF THE YEAR

Samhain

On my social media pages I know how many of you just *love* Samhain/Halloween. At least a month before, my feed becomes peppered with trick-or-treat outfit suggestions, pumpkin spice recipes, Jack-o'-lantern carving examples and, best of all, more and more people talking about divination techniques and talking with the ancestors.

All very fun and cool . . . and then the real job starts: the myth busting! All of the real witches start trying to educate folks that Hallowe'en isn't a modern American festival; that it's not just about dress-ups and that there is a deeper message.

Samhain is an ancient Celtic festival linked to winter and death. In the traditional time it's held, the season is moving towards winter and the dying back of earthly energy. Its origins reflect the fact that winter would indeed be a time when death would stalk people, animals and plants. In places where the temperatures could drop to below freezing on a regular basis, this meant death was a real possibility and so was going hungry, as food may not be so available. Death in these times was visible, intimate, common even. Everyone would have seen a death or probably had a death in their family and death happened at home, not in some institution like a hospital.

Death, then, was part of life. Samhain allows the exploration of death in a safe way. Trick or treating allows us to dress up and disguise ourselves from the naughty, returning spirits and wander happily and incognito with our ancestors and other benevolent spirits.

Witches see Samhain as an incredibly profound and powerful time – in fact, it's considered our Witches' New Year. I personally see this time as the fallow or void time, full of possibility of things to come rather than as a time for sorrow or fear.

HOW TO CELEBRATE SAMHAIN

Most witches I know have a special dinner where we cook up a feast, invite our like-minded friends and leave a place for the 'honoured dead'. Those who have passed are invited to join us in spirit form and party along with us.

Of course, there is trick or treating, and powerful oracular work can be performed on this night!

2 Monday

Waning

3 Tuesday

Waning

4 Wednesday

Waning

Wednesday is named after the Norse god Wodin (Odin).

5 Thursday

Waning

6 Friday 🌗

Waning

7 Saturday 🌗

Waning

8 Sunday 🌗

Waning

The stag appears
Within the forest circle
It calls for its own wildness and immortality...

- THE GODDESS

OCTOBER

M	T	W	T	F	S	S
						1
2	**3**	**4**	**5**	**6**	**7**	**8**
9	10	11	12	13	14	15
16	17	18	19	20	21	22
23	24	25	26	27	28	29
30	31					

9 Monday ◐

Waning

10 Tuesday ◐

Waning

11 Wednesday ◐

Waning

12 Thursday ◐

Waning

13 Friday ●

Dark moon

Exercise extreme self-care. Make this a night just for you and your nourishment.

14 Saturday ☽ New moon in Libra 1.55 pm EDT

A moon that assists with the healing of nasty relationships and one that assists us to be both more diplomatic but to hold necessary boundaries.

15 Sunday ◑

Waxing

OCTOBER

M	T	W	T	F	S	S
						1
2	3	4	5	6	7	8
9	**10**	**11**	**12**	**13**	**14**	**15**
16	17	18	19	20	21	22
23	24	25	26	27	28	29
30	31					

16 Monday ◐

Waxing

17 Tuesday ◐

Waxing

18 Wednesday ◐

Waxing

19 Thursday ◐

Waxing

20 Friday 🌓

Waxing

21 Saturday 🌓

Waxing

22 Sunday 🌓

Waxing

Create! Blossom!

This is your birthright.

- THE GODDESS

OCTOBER						
M	T	W	T	F	S	S
						1
2	3	4	5	6	7	8
9	10	11	12	13	14	15
16	**17**	**18**	**19**	**20**	**21**	**22**
23	24	25	26	27	28	29
30	31					

23 Monday

Waxing

24 Tuesday

Waxing

25 Wednesday

Waxing

26 Thursday

Waxing

27 Friday ◐

Waxing

28 Saturday ○ Full moon in Taurus 4.24 pm EDT

Get moving. A moon to help you get unstuck. If you suffer from negative procrastination, here is the moon to cast with to banish this!

Penumbral lunar eclipse seen from New York.

29 Sunday ◑

Waning

NOVEMBER

- What would I like to create, experience and manifest this month?

_____

_____

_____

_____

- What are the important dates for me this month?

_____

_____

- What would give me joy this month?

_____

_____

- What am I devoted to?

_____

_____

- Ideas, musings, actions:

_____

_____

_____

LAKSHMI

The Hindu goddess of wealth, light and general prosperity is lotus-sitting Lakshmi (Sanskrit: लक्ष्मी, lakṣmī, ˈləkʃmi).

Long haired, golden skinned and dressed in red, she is commonly depicted surrounded by two royal elephants showering her with a flow of abundant water, and she has a shower of gold coins flowing from her hands. I always notice how her expression is invariably calm, graceful and benevolent – sometimes the opposite of what we feel around prosperity issues such as money and our own finances.

Although Lakshmi is worshipped by millions every day, her biggest festival is that of Diwali, the festival of lights, which is around 12 November in India this year. I have been privileged to be part of a Diwali celebration in rural Rajasthan in India, and it was so very moving and inspiring.

On this full moon, oil lamps and candles are lit in every home and particularly inside and outside every shop and business. The lights are to honour the goddess but also to draw her to the place for her blessing of prosperity. Everything is tidied and cleaned thoroughly and the doors and windows to all the shops are left open; even the safes are left empty and wide so that Lakshmi can visit and bring with her the energy of wealth and plenty. New clothes are worn and feasting follows the goddess's visit.

You too can ask for Lakshmi's blessing at any time and you don't need to wait for Diwali.

Spell for Prosperity

Many of you have asked me to include this spell for prosperity working with Lakshmi after a few years ago when you had such success with it. I am happy to! A reminder: if you don't have a bath you can do this with a large bowl, and instead of bathing in it you can take it with you into the shower and pour it upon yourself.

Gather: at least five tea lights • a handful of rice, *(jasmine or basmati is nice)* • a cup of full-cream milk rose petals or lotus seeds • three large denomination coins *(Australian $2 are perfect)*.

Run the bath *(or prepare the large bowl by filling it with warm water)*.

Light all the tea lights, and as you do say:

'Great goddess Lakshmi, you who take joy in wealth and abundance, hear my prayer. Light the way for better prosperity now and for this year.'

Disrobe. Just before entering the water throw in the rice and say:

'I offer this rice to you as a symbol of abundance and good harvest.'

Add the cup of milk and say:

'I offer this milk to you, Lakshmi, as a symbol of wealth and plenty.'

Add the flower petals or seeds and say:

'I offer these flowers/seeds to you, Lakshmi, as a celebration of what is to come!'

Get into the bath (or place your hands into the bowl).

Relax. Take the coins in your hand and imagine having all the prosperity that you could want. Imagine having the financial and work goals that you have set yourself. This very positive feeling is something Lakshmi loves! Imagine infusing the coins with this feeling.

Then say: *'Lakshmi, bless these coins as talismans of prosperity. I offer them to you and charge them with attraction!'*

Put them in the bath (or bowl). Luxuriate in your bath of abundance! (If you are using the bowl, now have a shower and pour the contents on yourself.)

Thank Lakshmi and dry off. Take the coins and put two in places where you need prosperity e.g. your purse, wallet, by the phone or computer, at work.

The third coin you should spend or place in the ocean to spread Lakshmi's blessing.

30 Monday

Waning

31 Tuesday

Waning

It's Samhain! Happy Witches' New Year!

This is the celebration of seeing death as just another part of life. This is one of the two nights of the year when the veils between the worlds are at their thinnest, so it is a great night for divination of all kinds. Feast with your friends and don't forget those who have passed – set a place for them, pour them wine, leave them delicious food and speak about them!

1 Wednesday

Waning

2 Thursday

Waning

3 Friday ●

Waning

4 Saturday ●

Waning

5 Sunday ●

Waning

OCTOBER							NOVEMBER						
M	T	W	T	F	S	S	M	T	W	T	F	S	S
						1			1	2	3	4	5
2	3	4	5	6	7	8	6	7	8	9	10	11	12
9	10	11	12	13	14	15	13	14	15	16	17	18	19
16	17	18	19	20	21	22	20	21	22	23	24	25	26
23	24	25	26	27	28	29	27	28	29	30			
30	31												

6 Monday ◐

Waning

7 Tuesday ◐

Waning

8 Wednesday ◐

Waning

9 Thursday ◐

Waning

10 Friday ◖

Waning

11 Saturday ◑

Waning

Harvest below-ground fruits and vegetables now.

12 Sunday ●

Dark moon

Cut cords with events, people or relationships that no longer serve you or support your future.

Settle a little,
Build that foundation
Go deep, and then
Grow strong.

– THE GODDESS

NOVEMBER

M	T	W	T	F	S	S
		1	2	3	4	5
6	**7**	**8**	**9**	**10**	**11**	**12**
13	14	15	16	17	18	19
20	21	22	23	24	25	26
27	28	29	30			

13 Monday ☽ New moon in Scorpio 4.27 am EST

Know your worth. Set intentions for your growth and strength.

14 Tuesday ◑

Waxing

15 Wednesday ◑

Waxing

16 Thursday ◑

Waxing

17 Friday ◐

Waxing

18 Saturday ◐

Waxing

19 Sunday ◐

Waxing

NOVEMBER

M	T	W	T	F	S	S
			1	2	3	4	5
6	7	8	9	10	11	12
13	**14**	**15**	**16**	**17**	**18**	**19**
20	21	22	23	24	25	26
27	28	29	30			

20 Monday ◑

Waxing

21 Tuesday ◑

Waxing

22 Wednesday ◑

Waxing

23 Thursday ◑

Waxing

24 Friday ☽

Waxing

25 Saturday ☽

Waxing

Trim your hair now if you wish to encourage growth.

26 Sunday ☽

Waxing

NOVEMBER

M	T	W	T	F	S	S
		1	2	3	4	5
6	7	8	9	10	11	12
13	14	15	16	17	18	19
20	**21**	**22**	**23**	**24**	**25**	**26**
27	28	29	30			

DECEMBER

◆ What would I like to create, experience and manifest this month?

_____

_____

_____

_____

◆ What are the important dates for me this month?

_____

_____

◆ What would give me joy this month?

_____

_____

◆ What am I devoted to?

_____

_____

◆ Ideas, musings, actions:

_____

_____

_____

WINTER

There are diehard winter lovers out there, people who live for the cool, cold, snow and ice. These people are often grumpy in summer and complain about the heat and dream about gentler times in front of a fire all cocooned up.

This cocooning and withdrawal is completely natural because winter is our extreme season for introversion. As much as summer is the brash, let's-get-out-there, extroverted flipside, winter is the deeper, dreamier and, if we allow it, more restorative time.

Earth-wise, the shorter days and lower temperatures pause growth. Depending upon where you live, winter can mean you don't even see the soil for months on end, let alone plant life, due to metres of snow. This coating of ice allows a dieback, a gentle withdrawal into fallowness. Everything slows, and if we are open to this we could even say the earth has a little sleep.

And what of us – we humans? Are we not part of this great circle too? I think winter is an opportunity to align with the cycles and find some relief in slowing down a little. We can be a bit more inward facing, perhaps a bit more self-examining. We might choose to spend more solitary time with ourselves and our projects. We might sit back and allow ourselves to dream a little (or a lot) and certainly we can each forward plan. I personally do a lot of planning and exploration of the possibility of new projects in winter. I write of course still, but winter always signals for me to enjoy the playful 'what if?' without having to action it all way too quickly.

This, though, doesn't mean we do nothing and sit on the couch all day. Movement is important in winter too because we do not wish to invite in stagnancy. Bracing walks outside, experiencing the extremes of weather safely, eating well for the season, keeping our body warm and stimulated are super important in this extreme season.

For those of you who love to work with gods and goddesses, the long nights are a great time to work with those that are considered 'dark'. Working with our shadow side, having the courage to transform what no longer works for us is rewarding work to do now. Also playing with the energies of deities who are of or rule over winter and its elements is rewarding. If you ski, bless your skis by throwing a little snow over them and asking for Ullr's blessing (the Norwegian ski team do!).

Snow blessing with Ullr

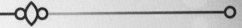

Ullr is the Norse god of snow, the bow and mountains. He was an admired warrior and the Edda refers to him as being good in a duel. He is also responsible for the invention of skis – so for those of you who love to frolic in the snow and engage in snow sports, Ullr is your god guy!

Every season when I have access to snow *(and that's not always easy where I come from)* I make sure I ask Ullr's assistance in blessing my skis and snow gear. Yes, everything from my snowshoes, skins, beacon, clothing, backpack – pretty much anything I'll use while I'm out in the snow and ice.

Before I go out or leave for a trip, I put everything outside on the grass or a table and I say:

'Great Ullr! Master bowman, expert outdoorsman, inventor of skis: I ask you to bless my equipment and keep me safe.'

I then offer Ullr a glass of good cider or mead. I pour this on the ground or leave it on my altar. I save the last sip for myself because the Norse gods appreciate us having a drink with them! Skol!

Then when I get to the snow, I place my skis or snowshoes upright in the snow before putting them on to ski or wear for the first time, and I again ask for Ullr's blessing and dedicate my first day to him.

I do this by throwing some snow on the equipment and saying:

'Ullr! Bless these skis/snowshoes/snow board/ice skates [whatever you have]. *Allow me to be skillful and enjoy this day, which I dedicate to you!'*

AMUN

GOD OF THE MONTH – DECEMBER

Amun is one of the eight primordial elemental Egyptian deities. He is the god of air. Referred to as the 'hidden one' or the 'invisible one', he is a creator god. He is depicted as having two feathered plumes on his head, carrying an ankh and a 'was' sceptre.

He was considered a champion of those with no voice and the preferred god of the poor or 'everyman' in Egyptian society. He is therefore a popular god to pray to for help for justice, against unfairness and for those who lack power.

Certain pharaohs attributed their victories over foreign invaders like the Hyksos to him and, as such, he was considered a protector of the realm. He was the god who protected those on the road, traders and those who had to travel to foreign places.

Amun is a god who it is said required virtue of his worshippers and it is more likely he will answer your petition if you have cleansed yourself of bad deeds and engaged in merciful good deeds. Amun knows your heart, and if it is heavy with negative deeds then why would he turn your way?

Like many deities, Amun's aspect and role evolved over time and circumstances and at the whim of the pharaoh. For example, during the Middle Kingdom he became the king of all the deities. During the New Kingdom he became a nationally worshipped god, and so had a cult everywhere in the kingdom. Later, as he became even higher in importance and the Egyptian kingdom expanded, he merged with Ra, the ancient solar god who was already worshipped in these new territories, to become Amun-Ra.

Today, more than ever, the idea of a god who speaks for those who cannot speak for themselves is a powerful one. A god who can assist with justice and protection of those with little visibility is a god of hope we need in the world right now.

INVOCATION FOR PROTECTION FOR ALL

AT THIS TIME OF YEAR, SENDING OUT POSITIVE ENERGY TO ALL THAT WILL RECEIVE IT SEEMS LIKE A GOOD IDEA. I LIKE TO DO THIS INVOCATION IN A QUIET SPACE OUTSIDE IN THE SUN WITH NO DISTRACTIONS. TURN YOUR PHONE OFF. I ALSO LIKE TO DO THIS SOMEWHERE HIGH WITH A VIEW IF POSSIBLE AS IT'S EASIER TO IMAGINE SENDING OUT POSITIVE ENERGY TO THE WORLD.

Breathe deeply. Centre. Connect your sit bones
or feet with the earth. Breathe again.

Light some incense if you wish, but this is not necessary.

Take a deep breath. Close your eyes. Imagine being on a
high point overlooking the Nile River or the desert.

THEN SAY:

'Creator of all things and merciful one, Amun, I call upon you humbly.

*'I call upon the creative spark, the flow of the waters, the wind in the sky,
the air that I breathe, this sweet burning of incense. I gather all up in
your name and ask for it all to be blessed by you and sent out in virtue.
I ask that you lend your energy of protection to all who need it.'*

Imagine Amun now in your presence in whatever way you
wish. There is no one perfect vision or way. Amun now lends
you his energy. Combine it with yours and send it out!

Imagine a flow of vital power full of love, justice and protection being sent out to
every single being willing to receive it. Send it out. Send it out widely and deeply.

Stay in this feeling and sending out as long as you like.

When you are ready, open your eyes. Thank Amun for his energy and blessings.

If you were standing, lift one foot and then the other to unplug.

CLAP THREE TIMES AND SAY:

'It is done.'

WHEEL OF THE YEAR

Yule

21 DECEMBER 10.27 PM EST

If you have ever spent any time around Christmas in Europe or Scandinavia, you'll appreciate that Yule (Yul) is a living and breathing tradition. Yule, though, is a pre-Christian celebration so Christmas got its roots in the Yule traditions. Yule is an ancient solstice festival celebrating the return of the light after the longest night of the year. This highlights the idea of a birth of light and hope over darkness, as from this night onwards the daylight hours will grow a tiny increment each day and eventually the warmth will return to the earth.

This hope of getting through the worst of the winter is survival stuff! Food was often scarce; there was little hunting to be had; the cold could pick off elder members of the society; and even wood for the fire was hard to get . . . In short, winter was a harsh and dangerous time.

So back to our symbology – the tree brings nature inside, the gift giving is the joy and happiness of surviving another season and the gratitude of fecundity-returning magical talismans for good luck and prosperity are created on this night and given as presents to those we love. The famous Yule log is covered in wishes for the future and ritually burnt to release those intentions. In ancient times, all the fires in the village were lit from this one flame. The ashes are highly magical and can be used in other workings later in the year.

HOW TO CELEBRATE YULE

Weeks before Yule, many witches make handmade or hand-grown presents for their family and friends. This need not be expensive. I make potions and bath salts and talismans for my loved ones, for example, and all are made with tonnes of magic and gratitude.

I decorate my altar with greens and golds, lots of sparkly candles and sweet incense such as frankincense, pine and myrrh. I make a powerful spiced mulled wine and I also make Yule cookies with little fortunes written in piped icing sugar on the underside. I have a garden with some big trees so I don't do a Yule tree inside, but choose to decorate a live tree outside with ribbons, solar-powered lights and handmade decorations.

Then I will pick out the important Yule log. This can be preferably a branch or section of wood that a tree has discarded. Prepare some small slips of paper for you and your guests to write their hopeful wishes upon. Pin these on the log, then burn the log to release the wishes while giving a cheer!

27 Monday ○ Full moon in Gemini 4.16 am EST

A little structure is not a bad thing! We are almost at the end of 2023, so you might like to use this lunar event to lightly plan your next moves.

28 Tuesday ◗

Waning

29 Wednesday ◗

Waning

30 Thursday ◗

Waning

1 Friday ◐

Waning

2 Saturday ◐

Waning

3 Sunday ◐

Waning

NOVEMBER							DECEMBER						
M	T	W	T	F	S	S	M	T	W	T	F	S	S
		1	2	3	4	5					1	2	3
6	7	8	9	10	11	12	4	5	6	7	8	9	10
13	14	15	16	17	18	19	11	12	13	14	15	16	17
20	21	22	23	24	25	26	18	19	20	21	22	23	24
27	28	29	30				25	26	27	28	29	30	31

4 Monday ◑

Waning

5 Tuesday ◑

Waning

6 Wednesday ◑

Waning

7 Thursday ◑

Waning

8 Friday ◑

Waning

9 Saturday ◑

Waning

10 Sunday ◑

Waning

Feel every cell
Alive
Sparkling
Yours and mine
Cosmic, immortal, delicious.

- THE GODDESS

DECEMBER

M	T	W	T	F	S	S
				1	2	3
4	**5**	**6**	**7**	**8**	**9**	**10**
11	12	13	14	15	16	17
18	19	20	21	22	23	24
25	26	27	28	29	30	31

11 Monday ●

Dark moon

The last dark moon for the year. Relax, take some solo time and do the last of the year's shadow workings tonight.

12 Tuesday ☽ New moon in Sagittarius 6.32 pm EST

Enjoy this last new moon for 2023! It's a friendly new moon, which is perfect to set intentions for pleasure and freedom.

13 Wednesday ◐

Waxing

14 Thursday ◐

Waxing

15 Friday

Waxing

16 Saturday

Waxing

17 Sunday

Waxing

Observe.
Look about you.

– THE GODDESS

DECEMBER

M	T	W	T	F	S	S
				1	2	3
4	5	6	7	8	9	10
11	**12**	**13**	**14**	**15**	**16**	**17**
18	19	20	21	22	23	24
25	26	27	28	29	30	31

18 Monday ◑

Waxing

19 Tuesday ◑

Waxing

20 Wednesday ◑

Waxing

21 Thursday ◑ Yule, winter solstice 10.27 am EST

Waxing

Happy Yule! This solstice reflects the shortest day of the year and the longest night. Hope breaks through the darkness! It is a traditional feasting time and one of the best times to make charms and talismans for abundance. Make delicious mulled wine and burn a Yule log with your wishes attached.

22 Friday ◐

Waxing

23 Saturday ◐

Waxing

24 Sunday ◐

Waxing
Christmas Eve.

You are part of a great whole.
Important and integral.
Beloved.
Needed.
Enjoyed.

- THE GODDESS

DECEMBER

M	T	W	T	F	S	S
				1	2	3
4	5	6	7	8	9	10
11	12	13	14	15	16	17
18	**19**	**20**	**21**	**22**	**23**	**24**
25	26	27	28	29	30	31

25 Monday

Waxing

Christmas Day.

26 Tuesday ○ Full moon in Cancer 7.33 pm EST

Go outside and give this moon a big howl as it's the last of 2023. A perfect moon to do spellcraft to support your health, energy and vitality.

27 Wednesday

Waning

28 Thursday

Waning

29 Friday

Waning

30 Saturday

Waning

31 Sunday

Waning

It's the final night of this year, so ride the positive wave of wishes for the new year! Take a big breath in and out and mark the moment with a kiss, a dance or a sip of champagne! Spill a little on the ground for the goddess of the new year, Jana, as the clock goes to midnight.

Check Stacey Demarco on Facebook for the free annual Ride the Wave Ritual Event. Let go of what was and ready yourself for new momentum! Ensure you have your intentions set for 2024. Mark the end of this year with a ritual of gratitude before you head out to celebrate.

DECEMBER

M	T	W	T	F	S	S
				1	2	3
4	5	6	7	8	9	10
11	12	13	14	15	16	17
18	19	20	21	22	23	24
25	**26**	**27**	**28**	**29**	**30**	**31**

NOTES AND MUSINGS

REORDER FOR 2024 LUNAR DIARY

Name..

Address...

City....................................State.....................

Postcode....................Country......................

Phone...

Email..

Mastercard ☐   Visa ☐

Credit card number..

Name on card...

Expiry date: ....CVV number............

Please send me .... copies of

2024 Lunar Diary

USD$19.95 / GBP £18.99 per copy

To place an order in the USA
Red Wheel/Weiser/Conari
65 Parker Street, Suite 7
Newburyport, MA 01950, USA
Toll Free: 800.423.7087
orders@rwwbooks.com

To place an order in the UK
Simon and Schuster UK
1st Floor
222 Gray's Inn Road
London WC1X8HB
United Kingdom
Tel: +44 (0)20 7316 1900
Fax: +44 (0)20 7316 0332
enquiries@simonandschuster.co.uk

2023 MOON PHASES

UNIVERSAL TIME CHART

If you don't live in the USA and don't wish to convert times from New York timings, here is a handy chart that gives moon phases in Universal Time (UT). It is the mean solar time for the meridian at Greenwich, England, used as a basis for calculating time throughout most of the world.

DARK MOON	NEW MOON	FULL MOON
–	–	6 January, 11.07 pm
20 January	21 January, 8.53 pm	5 February, 6.28 pm
19 February	20 February, 7.05 am	7 March, 12.40 pm
20 March	21 March, 5.23 pm	6 April, 4.34 am
19 April	20 April, 4.12 am	5 May, 5.34 pm
18 May	19 May, 3.53 pm	4 June, 3.41 am
17 June	18 June, 4.37 am	3 July, 11.38 am
16 July	17 July, 6.31 pm	1 August, 6.31 pm
15 August	16 August, 9.38 am	31 August, 8.31 am
14 September	15 September, 1.39 am	29 September, 9.57 am
13 October	14 October, 5.55 pm	28 October, 8.24 pm
12 November	13 November, 9.27 am	27 November, 9.16 am
11 December	12 December, 11.32 pm	27 December, 12.33 am

RESOURCES

Here is a list of handy moon, earth and pagan-related resources that I particularly like.

The Pagan Awareness Network

www.paganawareness.net.au: if you want more information on paganism or witchcraft this is a great place to start. The Pagan Awareness Network Incorporated (PAN Inc) is a not-for-profit educational association with members Australia-wide. It is directed by a management committee whose members are drawn from a broad cross-section of the pagan community. It has no formal ties with any religious body, but works proactively both within the pagan community and as a point of contact for the public, including government and media organisations. PAN Inc aims to continue as the Australian pagan community's most effective networking and educational body.

www.themodernwitch.com: this is my website and contains loads of free resources, witches' tools, free downloads and also a store from which you can obtain books, downloads, blessed talismans and temple beads including lunar beads. Register for the free newsletter!

www.natureluster.com: this is my site about the benefits and wonders of an earth-centred life. Try the Natureluster Programme. Search for Natureluster on Instagram.

LUNAR WEBSITES

* *http://eclipse.gsfc.nasa.gov/phase/phasecat.html:* yes, it's a NASA site giving a great history and current info about moon phases. Wonderful for researching your lunar return.
* *www.timeanddate.com:* great for lunar timing/equinox info.

TIDAL INFORMATION

Strangely enough some of the best tidal information comes from your popular newspapers e.g. in Australia: *The Sydney Morning Herald, The Age.*

Try *www.smh.com.au* OR *www.theage.com.au.*

For moon gardening: *www.green-change.com* OR *www.moongardeningcalendar.com.*

CONNECT WITH ME

Connect with Stacey Demarco: *www.facebook.com/staceydemarco*

Stacey Demarco's Lunar & Seasonal Diary Page:
www.facebook.com/groups/463439380369917

Instagram: *The Modern Witch*

If you are interested there are many fan pages set up for gods and goddesses that you can join.

ABOUT THE AUTHOR

Stacey Demarco is The Modern Witch. Passionate about bringing practical magic to everyone and inspiring people to have a deeper connection with nature, Stacey has been teaching witchcraft and mythos for many decades. This diary is now in its 13th edition and is published in both the southern and northern hemispheres.

She is the author of the bestsellers *Witch in the Boardroom*, *Witch in the Bedroom* and *The Enchanted Moon* – all translated into other languages. She is the co-writer of *The No Excuses Guide to Soulmates*, *The No Excuses Guide to Purpose* and *Plants of Power*. Her oracle card decks include the bestselling *Queen of the Moon*, *Divine Animals*, *Moon Magick* and *The Elemental Oracle* – all illustrated by Kinga Britschgi.

Stacey is the founder of Natureluster, which educates and works to reconnect people to the health-giving power of nature.

An animal activist, ethical beekeeper and dedicated adventure traveller, she lives in Sydney on a cliff by the beach with her husband and furry companions. Stacey provides private consults as well as teaching workshops and leads the popular Wild Souls Retreats nationally and internationally.

Learn more at *www.themodernwitch.com*.